Part-Time, Please!

Part-Time, Please!

From maternity leave back to work:
A mum's guide to negotiation and re-integration

MARIANNE FERNANDEZ

authorHOUSE®

AuthorHouse™ UK Ltd.
1663 Liberty Drive
Bloomington, IN 47403 USA
www.authorhouse.co.uk
Phone: 0800.197.4150

Published by AuthorHouse   05/22/2013

ISBN: 978-1-4817-9106-9 (sc)
ISBN: 978-1-4817-9109-0 (e)

About the Author

Despite her exotic sounding name Marianne Fernández is Welsh. Having graduated from university with a business degree she embarked upon a successful career in various multinational companies. Like many women today, Marianne became a mother once her career was well established, at the age of 36. She understands the demands of the corporate world from the perspective of both a senior manager and a working mum and this brings balance to her work as an author, trainer and speaker.

Marianne lives in rural Wiltshire with her family. She can be contacted via her website www.optimums.co.uk and would love to hear from you.

Acknowledgments

I would like to thank several people who have contributed significantly to the completion of this book. Thanks go to Gill Simpson, Hélène Cooper, Caroline Tye and Dr Laura Lafave who each provided encouragement and challenge in equal measure and gave their time generously in the editing and review process.

Enormous thanks to the mums whose published interviews provide this book with colour, emotion and realism.

Thanks also to the many mums whose interviews, although not published, provided re-enforcement to the main messages in the book.

Thanks to the managers who confidentially and candidly offered their views and shared how the return to work experience feels from the other side of the desk. Your input adds balance to the content.

Many thanks to the team at AuthorHouse who ensured a smooth publication process for this first time author.

Finally I would like to thank my wonderful husband, Albert, whose patience and support have enabled me to cross the finish line.

For Ania

"my beautiful and my best"

Contents

Introduction

Congratulations on becoming a mum! According to the Office for National Statistics 808,000 babies were born in the UK in 2011. Various studies have shown that roughly 65% of mums go back to work after childbirth, so we can estimate that an impressive 525,000 women rejoined the UK workforce at some point in 2012! That's a lot of women going through a lot of change – and it happens every year!

I had my own much longed for daughter in summer 2009. As a professional woman I always knew I wanted to go back to work part-time after my maternity leave and I was in that mindset from the start of my pregnancy. What struck me as I went through the experience was the lack of guidance available to help me through the return to work process. As my maternity leave came to an end I realised I didn't feel at all informed in a number of important areas and six big questions stood out in particular:

- how to get peace of mind about leaving my baby in childcare
- how to regain my professional confidence
- what part-time working pattern to ask for
- how to negotiate part-time working with my employer
- how to embrace becoming a working mum and make it a positive experience
- what to do if my employer rejected my application to work part-time

Since early 2010 I have sought to better understand the life-changing transition to becoming a working mum. I have interviewed scores of women in both the private and public sector and had very useful conversations with managers in a variety of industries. I have become trained in maternity law, gained a coaching qualification and designed a successful post maternity re-integration support programme that I now offer through my company, OptiMums.

This book will help you in all the areas identified above and enable you to approach your own return to work in a well informed, proactive and professional manner. You have some important decisions to make and, if this is your first baby, a big life change to adjust to but you are not alone. It will be my pleasure to share your journey with you and pass on what I have learned as a result of my own, far from perfect, return to work experience and subsequent research and training development. The goal of this book is to enable you to feel supported, think broader and plan your own return to work effectively. This is not designed to be a self-help book that you read in order to temporarily lift your mood. Used fully this book will provide you with tangible end results and you will have created and negotiated your personal return to work solution.

A few notes about terminology before we get started. As I researched the book it became apparent that when mums talk to each other they use the term 'part-time' to describe their working pattern even if it also includes elements such as home working, shift work or flexible hours. Throughout the book I have therefore used 'part-time' in the same umbrella manner.

I'm sure you recognise the term 'flexible working request'. It is the formal description for an application to change the terms of a contract of employment. It isn't a term that mums use everyday when they talk to each other however. Most of us announce,

"I've asked to work part-time."

So I have therefore used the phrase 'part-time working request' in place of 'flexible working' in most areas because it is a better fit with the context and tone of the book.

As you get started don't worry if you only get a few spare minutes here and there to read. I recognise that it is unlikely that you will be able to get through this book in just a few sittings. In recognition of this I will end each chapter with a summary of key points. This will help if you are interrupted, sleep deprived, short of time or a mum who, like me, finds a quick recap helps to solidify learning before moving on to the next topic.

Just as each one of us is an individual with different family situations and different jobs, each return to work solution will be unique. Some aspects of this book may be helpful and others less so. That's fine. Take what works for you and disregard what doesn't.

For those of you reading a paper version of this book I would encourage you to use it as a notepad rather than simply a read. Please feel free to grab a pen or a highlighter and scribble in the margins or underline whatever you find most helpful as you go along. There is a baby in your house after all so this book will probably be chewed, dribbled on and crawled over in no time anyway! Go and find whatever you need and let's get started!

PART 1

I'm dreading going back!

Am I alone?

You are never alone!

It is quite normal to feel emotional as you start to think about the end of your maternity leave. Most women feel apprehensive about going back to work and the longer you have been on maternity leave the more likely you are to feel anxious and unsettled as it draws to an end. Various reports have been written and studies made to support what most women already know – going back to work after having a baby can be tough, especially if you have just had your first baby and this is your first experience of becoming a working mum. To further highlight that you are not alone I'd like to share a little of my own return to work experience and how I came to write this book.

The mystery of the good return to work experience

I love a good murder mystery and in order to track down answers to the six questions I mentioned in the Introduction I approached the lack of information like a 'whodunnit', or to be more precise, 'whodunnit well'! I was still on maternity leave at the time and I'd probably been watching too much daytime TV!

Back in 2010 I never did find the role model or helping hand that I was looking for in time for my own return to work and consequently the experience was not one I'd like to repeat. However, travelling life's bumpy roads can teach you more than having a smooth easy ride and I was determined to understand what I could have done differently to get a better result. My desire to have a second baby was great motivation because I wanted to enjoy a radically better return to work next time.

My sleuth-like investigations continued after I went back to work and I started asking every working mum I met, both inside and outside of my workplace, about their experience. I quickly discovered that I wasn't alone. One mum confided:

> "Going back to work was difficult because
> I really didn't know what I was supposed to
> do. I didn't get any help about asking for
> part-time work or any support when I did
> go back in those first few weeks. My family
> and friends were sympathetic but I still
> felt pretty much left to get on with it on my
> own. It was quite lonely actually."

The comments I got from my network up and down the country, from mums working in the public or private sector, indicated the same problem. Mums don't ask for support when they go back to work because they don't know what support to ask for. Sound familiar?

I also started to share my experience with middle and senior managers in various industries who had been responsible for re-integrating new mums back into their teams and that was really enlightening. One Regional Director admitted,

> "We tend to fiddle our way through
> re-inductions after maternity leave."

Another Head of Department, who had seen four women from his team go on maternity leave and return in quick succession, was equally honest.

> "My approach to their return to work was
> quite haphazard and I probably handled the
> situation differently with each of them. If
> I got anything right or wrong I don't really
> know what that was or why."

My enquiries highlighted that many managers don't know what help to offer and as every mum is different, and may want something different by way of support, a one-size-fits-all approach is unlikely to work. Added to this is the fact that most line managers in the UK have no maternity law or flexible working legislation training and it's not surprising that it feels like a challenge for all concerned. As a consequence many mums returning to work get less support than they need and managers are inwardly aware that this is the case. Despite this no one seems to know how to improve the situation, so it keeps repeating itself.

By this point I felt as though I could stop my sleuthing. I was starting to understand the root causes of the problem, why there was a lack of information and how the problems could be broken down and addressed. So what do I recommend as the solution?

Three home cooked return to work recipes

During my own maternity leave, while my baby was sleeping, I learned to make cupcakes. It was wonderfully relaxing and my home smelled amazing while I was cooking. I was given a cupcake recipe book and it gave me confidence to experiment. You could see this book as your return to work recipe book because together we are going to make sure that you, as the chef, are properly equipped for the task and then you can try three easy to follow return to work recipes.

Well-balanced recipe 1: A Part-time Working Request

After reading this book you will be able to create a tempting part-time working request to rival any cupcake. You will be able to identify and carefully select the right ingredients for part-time working that appeal to both you and your manager. With a bit of guidance you will be able to bake it to perfection and present it beautifully. Your part-time working request needs to be well balanced and as attractive as possible so your manager can't help but say "Yes please!"

Energizing recipe 2: A Re-integration Support Proposal

Once your employer has agreed your part-time role we will go back to the kitchen to create another mouth watering offering akin to blending a fresh fruit smoothie, your re-integration support proposal.

This is a proposal created by you for your benefit. The proposal is sent by you to your manager <u>before</u> you go back to work. It will contain a number of performance enhancing support measures that you would appreciate during your first few weeks / months and has four significant benefits:

- it enables you to approach this key life transition in a proactive mindset and, with a little help from this book, create a personally tailored programme
- it provides you and your manager the opportunity to work together (after possibly a lengthy period) and collaborate on a topic of mutual interest i.e. your early high performance and ongoing engagement. This happens as you sit together <u>before</u> you return to work and agree which parts of your support proposal can be provided and will be put in place
- it noticeably reduces your stress before and during your return to work
- it helps both you and your manager to feel good about your imminent return knowing that you are getting the support you feel you need when you need it

This combination of benefits is surely energizing!

Calming recipe 3: A Home Support Plan

This third recipe is intended to give you peace of mind at home during those final few weeks and days of maternity leave so that you are better able to relax, sleep and enjoy remaining precious time with your baby.

This recipe will enable you to create your own personal home support plan with tips and suggestions on how you can help yourself and access the support of friends and family in those first few months back at work.

In cooking terms this is something simple, straightforward and warming like a bowl of soup on a cold day or a specially blended tea infusion that makes you inhale and exhale slowly as you wrap your hands around your mug. A well constructed home support plan will help reduce the looming sensation that many mums get as maternity leave draws to an end and turn it into a feeling of self assured readiness.

It is the creation of these three tangible items that makes this book more than just a feel-good read and we will come back to these recipes in more detail later.

Hopefully now you can see that it is normal for mums to feel daunted to some degree at the prospect of going back to work after maternity leave and managers often feel that they also lack guidance and support to handle the process well. In order to get an objective view of the situation let's spend a bit more time understanding how mums and managers experience the getting-ready-to-come-back-to-work process by joining two fictional but fact based characters Anna (a new mum) and Paul (Anna's manager) on a typical Monday morning.

A mum's perspective

Anna is a long-serving employee of Global Ltd and up until the birth of her son Daniel she worked normal office hours from Monday to Friday. Anna's maternity leave started during September and we join her 8 months later on a sunny day in May. Anna and Daniel are arriving at their local baby and toddler group. Daniel is now a solid 8 month old and Anna has had time to relax into her new role as a mum. Once inside the community centre she sees other mums getting out toys and shouts a friendly "Hello!" as she pushes Daniel in his pram to the unofficial buggy park. Finally she unburdens herself of her enormous ready-for-every-conceivable-situation baby bag and smiles with relief to have arrived for the start of the session.

Soon the playgroup is in full swing. The floor is strewn with colourful toys. A nursing mum is breastfeeding her infant in a misnamed 'quiet corner' on an equally misnamed 'comfy chair'. A semi-naked toddler is struggling successfully to avoid a much needed nappy change. A tired looking mum called Kate proudly announces that her daughter, Ella, cut her first tooth over the weekend. A pink cheeked Ella is busy chewing on Kate's mobile phone. Anna checks that Daniel is happy and safe on a play mat and wonders when he will cut his first tooth. Satisfied that he is content, she takes a seat nearby to watch him and enjoy her first hot cup of tea of the day. Kate flops into the chair next to Anna, offers her a biscuit and says.

"I'm shattered! Only got four hours sleep last night! Wow! Daniel is really growing! How old is he now?"
"8 months."
"Goodness, time flies doesn't it! When are you going back to work?"
"I planned to go back after 12 months maternity leave and I left the office in September, so I've been off nearly 9 months now. I suppose I need to start thinking about it fairly soon. I can't believe how fast it's gone!"

"I know! One minute they are tiny little things and the next they are crawling and sprouting teeth! Will you go back full or part-time?"

"Well, I worked full-time before Daniel was born but I'd prefer to go back part-time now, if they'll let me."

"What are you going to ask for?"

"I was thinking of asking for 3 days a week but I'm not sure which days to ask for and I'm not sure how to ask to be honest. I don't know what's happened to me since I had Daniel. It's as if the woman I used to be just vanished."

"Oh, that's Baby Brain!"

"Yeah, maybe."

"Well, good luck in your decision. Going back to work can be a bit tough to start with but you'll get through it."

"Thanks."

Kate dashes off to stop Ella using her new front tooth on a crayon.

The rest of Anna's time at Toddler group is spent playing with a heavy-eyed Daniel and talking with the other mums about the latest celebrities to become pregnant or have babies. Despite enjoying the trivia of celebrity gossip she keeps thinking about her need to get back in touch with the office. All too soon it's time to go home and Anna gently puts a sleeping Daniel into his car seat, loads the pram and throws her enormous baby bag into the passenger seat of her incredibly messy car. She sighs as she prepares to drive home wondering how she will approach this new phase of her life and how the last few months have flow by in a haze. This morning's brief chat has come as a bit of a wake up call and she needs to harness her thoughts as there are serious decisions to be made. As she drives home she thinks about her manager and asks herself:

- How do I talk to Paul about working part-time?

- What do I want to ask for exactly?

- If I have to do some negotiating, how do I do that?

- How will my going back to work affect Daniel?

- What will it be like to go back to work after so long away?

By the time Anna arrives home however her thoughts have moved on and she feels a mixture of emotions starting to build up. As she rummages in the bottom of her bag for her house keys she has a head full of unhelpful worries.

- What if I make the wrong childcare decision for Daniel and he is unhappy?

- What if I go back and I can't remember how to do my job?

- What if Paul and the team prefer the person who's been covering for me?

- What if that person has done a better job than me?

- What if, despite my best efforts, Paul says 'No'?

Anna is not alone in experiencing that sinking feeling as she contemplates everything involved in returning to work. Many mums do to some degree. Once you are in this return to work mindset you have mentally moved on from being a mum on maternity leave to being a soon-to-be working mum. Anna's conversation at playgroup highlights four common issues that many soon-to-be working mums encounter toward the end of maternity leave.

Four common challenges for a mum:
1) Negative emotions such as fear, dread and guilt.
2) Reduced professional self confidence and diminished self image (baby brain).
3) Knowledge gaps about flexible working legislation.
4) Not even considering asking for return to work support.

Let's take each one in turn and understand how these challenges can be addressed.

Common challenge for a mum no. 1: Negative emotions

As my own maternity leave came to an end I was plagued by a combination of fear, dread and guilt. I know how destructive these three emotions can be. Obviously I am not a medical doctor or a trained psychologist. What I share with you on this topic are ideas from a recognised author that I found personally helpful and my own strategies for combating these negative emotions.

Fear

My absolute favourite author on the topic of fear is Dr Susan Jeffers. Her book *Feel the Fear and Do It Anyway*® hits the spot and it comes in a humorous audio version *The Art of Fearbusting* that is perfect for listening to while you are driving or getting on with things around the house. Susan explains that everyone feels afraid when faced with something new.

> "Any time that you take a step in an unknown direction . . . you are going to feel fear."

> "The only way to get rid of the fear of doing something is . . . do it!"

As you read this you may feel fine, you may feel slightly anxious or you may be close to panic at the thought of going back to work and all it involves. It could be that you are worried about negotiating part-time working. It may be that actually going back to your workplace is creating anxiety. If you are concerned about negotiating then re-name it 'collaborating'. You will find lots of helpful practical ideas here to help you. Whatever the source of your worry and wherever you are on the fear spectrum Susan un-wraps fear down to its core by explaining that:

> "If we take it to the very bottom line, the fear you all have is that you won't be able to handle whatever life hands you."

She recommends the following positive affirmation repeated out loud over and over, her three magic words:

> "I'll handle it!"

Believe me, whatever it is about going back to work that is scaring you right now, you will handle it. I had a sticky note on the dashboard of my car with this little phrase on it, just to remind me during my commute. Sometimes I said it cheerily as I drove along with a smile on my face and other times I said it through gritted teeth with my hands clenched around the steering wheel. But I kept on saying it and I did handle it. Your fear is not going to go away until you face whatever it is that is frightening you but I can guarantee that, once you do face it, it will stop looming like a monster and shrink until it disappears altogether. In the meantime it is possible to be proactive despite your fear and enjoy life now. Trust me, within a few months of being back at work your fear will have gone and you will have handled it.

Dread

Dread is a thief. It steals your ability to focus on the joy of the here and now. It takes your attention away from your beautiful baby and instead it channels your energy into a daunting future full of ominous challenges. This was the sort of dread that gripped me and left me unable to really enjoy the last few precious months with my daughter before my return to work. As the end of maternity leave comes in sight it can be easy to become pre-occupied with thoughts about those first few days and weeks back at work and let a sinking feeling into your stomach and grey clouds gather around your head.

An effective antidote to dread is knowledge and preparation. This book will educate you about a life change that you may never have experienced before and enable you to take control and play a proactive part in your return to work. It is my sincere hope that as your levels of knowledge and personal influence increase your level of dread will reduce until it is barely registering or has turned a full 180 degrees into happy anticipation. This will allow you to spend your remaining maternity leave in the present moment, enjoying time with your baby.

Guilt

Guilt affects most working mothers to some extent and can show up on many different occasions during the return to work. What triggers guilt will vary from person to person. I had numerous guilt triggers but when I thought about them I found I could identify two voices of guilt. They were a bit like genres of music. Just as rock'n'roll gets your foot tapping and classical music can be soothing these two voices were very effective at pushing my emotional buttons and creating a gut wrenching response. I called them:

'How could you?' and 'Why can't you?'

Once I'd given these voices names I could then trace them back to my root fears and then deal with them objectively. Hopefully this will make more sense as you read on.

The 'How could you?' type of guilt was masterful at making me feel bad for doing something that I (apparently) shouldn't be doing such as:

- Putting my child in childcare.
- Wanting to attend to my career
- Enjoying being back at work
- Needing to be more than 100% mum
- Wanting some "me time"
- Staying later in the office to attend a meeting or finish a report

For me, the root fear was that I was being self-centred by not devoting myself entirely to the raising of my child.

Over time, as my hormones got back to normal and my confidence at work returned, I began to see that 'How could you?' accusations were actually based on incorrect thinking. There was nothing wrong with any of the things I was doing or enjoying or feeling a need for. In fact doing these things made me happier and more fulfilled as a person and that enriched my relationship with my baby girl. Due to the separation during the day I placed a higher value on the time we did spend together and I brought more energy and focus to our interaction and play time.

The 'Why can't you?' type of guilt regularly beat me up for not doing something I should (apparently) be doing for example:

- Not fitting into my pre-baby work clothes
- Not making time to home-cook every baby meal
- Not effectively juggling my old job and also be the perfect wife and mother
- Not having a clean and tidy home
- Not having a clean and tidy car
- Not being able to clean my daughter's new baby teeth, (she would not co-operate at all!)

The root fear here was that I was incapable and I simply didn't measure up. On reflection I came to see feelings associated with 'Why can't you?' were based on unrealistic expectations. I would not have expected anyone else to live up to the standards and ideals I was setting myself. I had to accept that, at this stage of my baby's life, I had to re-prioritise and distinguish what was important to do from what was now a nice-to-do. Compromise came quickly because I had to choose how to spend my time but reaching a better level of self acceptance took longer and can still be a struggle.

Once I could see that I was just doing the best I could day-to-day and that my choices were based on prioritising my daughter's wellbeing it became easier not to be perfect. It is still not easy even now and this is one area that I know I will need to continue to watch. The world expects us to do it all but it is just not possible.

When guilt crawls into your day it can be really hard to shake it off but do you really want your day to be spoiled by thoughts based on incorrect thinking or unrealistic expectations? Combating guilt takes determination and if you have that you are half way there. When you combine determination with a strategy, it becomes even more effective. I developed Guilt Squashers and here's how they worked for me.

Guilt Squashers

I have included below 3 scenarios that would regularly trigger my guilt in those first few weeks at work and the guilt squashers I employed to combat these thoughts before they took hold.

Scenario 1 - Dropping baby off at childcare before work

Guilty thought
"How can you leave your baby like this? This is precious time you are losing with her. How can you be so selfish? She needs you!"

Guilt squasher
My baby is well cared for in childcare and she is too young to even remember going. I know she cries initially when I drop her off but I know she always settles quickly once I've gone and has a good day. She always feeds well, gets lots of cuddles and is super smiley when I collect her. It is important for my well being and the family finances that I go to work.

Scenario 2 - Calling my childcare provider to tell them I'll be 30 minutes late collecting my baby because I need to stay at work to attend a meeting.

Guilty thought
"That's the second time this week! Your childcare provider will be really unimpressed with you doing this again. You're being selfish and taking advantage!"

Guilt squasher
My childcare provider has explained to me the extent of the extended childcare they can offer at short notice and I always operate within those pre agreed limits. Other parents do the same. Managing work and family requires that sometimes I stay a bit longer than my contracted hours to support my colleagues or finish a report and it is right that I do so.

Scenario 3 - Collecting baby later than usual and, as a result, having less time with her in the evening before bed time.

Guilty thought
"You are not spending enough time with your baby. You have got your priorities all wrong!"

Guilt squasher
I may occasionally spend less time at the end of my day with my baby as a result of working late but it does not happen often. I do not normally work late and my daughter is not suffering. She is grumpy because she is tired not because she has spent 30 minutes less time with me.

However you experience guilt it is important that you have a strategy to deal with it. It is unlikely to go away completely and it is a bit like one of the unwanted TV channels you get with your satellite TV package. You don't want it but you get it anyway. This rogue TV channel turns itself on every now and then and always at full volume so it grabs your attention.

You may not be able to get rid of it from the satellite TV menu but you can press the mute button or simply flick onto a more appealing channel. When guilt shows up – be in charge of the remote control!

Common challenge for a mum no. 2: Baby Brain

'Baby Brain' is a term that I came across during my own maternity leave. Mums used it to describe feelings of reduced personal effectiveness and lowered professional self-confidence.

Baby Brain seems to affect large numbers of mums and can be a bit of a shock to the first-time sufferer. You can start to wonder if you are losing the plot! You used to consider yourself confident and capable but you find you are extremely forgetful, have noticeably reduced professional self confidence and a voice in your head that is extremely critical of your appearance.

"How did this happen to me?" I hear you cry. I have a theory.

Everyone would accept that becoming a mum for the first time affects you in many different ways. During pregnancy, childbirth and maternity leave we can easily point out the physical, emotional, social and economic changes. Is it any wonder that many of us feel our mental capacity is also affected? Lets look at it a different way. Your morning routine before baby arrived used to look something like this:

1) wake up refreshed after an un-interrupted nights sleep
2) shower and prepare mentally for a meeting later today
3) dry and style hair
4) choose a smart, clean outfit
5) choose a different smarter outfit to impress in meeting

6) have quick, quiet breakfast
7) apply make up carefully and spritz perfume
8) select accessories
9) note that you have a dental appointment tomorrow
10) grab handbag containing keys, purse and mobile phone
11) go to work and take part in stimulating conversation

Your morning routine now that you are on maternity leave resembles something like this:

1) wake after a disrupted sleep with bags under eyes
2) feed baby, baby makes mess over you, him and the floor
3) wash and dress baby, change baby again 5 minutes later
4) eat breakfast one handed while comforting crying baby
5) put content baby in play pen with favourite toy
6) shower, enjoy 5 minutes of "me time" and try to wake up
7) dry hair, sort of style it and hope for the best
8) put on clean clothes (that just fit) then notice a baby stain
9) realise your Tesco Baby Club vouchers expired yesterday
10) spend an hour trying to tidy up the house, do the washing and entertain the baby with daytime TV in the background for company
11) spend 30 minutes preparing to leave the house with huge baby bag
12) attend Baby and Toddler group with other equally tired mums and talk about nothing remotely stimulating

Even though I know you wouldn't change it for the world the elements of your new routine can provide fertile ground for the seeds of self doubt to flourish. In my view, whatever the causes, the end result of Baby Brain is reduced self confidence (regarding your professional abilities) and diminished self image (beating yourself up over how you look).

If you are reading this and you think that you are suffering from Baby Brain, you probably are. Thankfully once you can recognise it and understand why you have it you can decide how to deal with it. That means making a conscious decision about what thoughts you decide to dwell upon and which thoughts you dismiss as being unhelpful and inaccurate.

Dr Susan Jeffers writes about what she calls "the Chatterbox" in each of our minds that "tries to drive us crazy. It is the repository of all our negative input" and it will undermine our self belief if we let it. Despite how you may feel, you are still the same person you were before you became a mum. Your professional strengths, skills and qualifications are still part of you. Just because you are temporarily not using them as much as you did before it does not mean they have vanished.

Susan suggests that when faced with this internal negativity and self doubt we need to keep repeating affirmative statements such as:

"I am an intelligent, capable, confident woman"

This strategy works because our subconscious mind takes on board what we say, even if we don't feel it.

Baby Brain's malicious thoughts are as real and as long-lasting as we let them be. They can be reduced to temporary little visitors from our "Chatterbox". Try using your imagination to visualise each unkind and incorrect thought as an ugly little character. As they come into your mind, treat them like uninvited and unwelcome guests. Imagine you have a 'thoughts sofa' and you are the one who decides which thoughts are allowed to sit there and occupy your mind. When these nasty little characters show up, show them the door.

When you feel yourself slipping into a negative thought pattern about your appearance or your competence, call a time-out and proactively build yourself up instead. Making an active effort to recall your strengths, abilities and qualifications isn't always easy because we don't often run an internal thought programme called:

"I am great!"

But starting to do exactly that will help to stop Baby Brain taking hold. Perhaps you can imagine your strengths and professional qualities as a series of pleasant characters and deliberately spend some time reminiscing with them instead. These important and valuable aspects of your previous life are just resting while you embrace a new and different learning curve of being a mum.

On an encouraging note, nearly every new mum I have spoken to has experienced the symptoms of Baby Brain to some degree and, despite their fears, they all re discovered their mental effectiveness when they went back to work and thereby restored their professional self confidence and improved their self image. You will too.

Common challenge for a mum no. 3:
Flexible working knowledge gaps

Anna mentioned not knowing how to ask her employer for part-time work and not being too sure what days to ask for. I have to admit that I was equally in the dark. In fact it wasn't until I got an initial letter from my employer rejecting my part-time working request and quoting a series of lengthy legal sounding reasons that it even occurred to me that there might be some legislation behind it all! That was a shock!

It is surprising how uninformed many of us are as we go through pregnancy, take maternity leave and then return to work. I've spoken with many intelligent professional women who admitted they felt quite clueless. Don't beat yourself up if this applies to you too because you are not alone and we will address your legal knowledge gaps on flexible working later in Part 1.

When it comes to agreeing part-time working, companies will differ. Some will have a published flexible working policy and others will not. If your employer has one, get a copy of it. If your employer does not have a flexible working policy, please don't jump to negative conclusions. It is not an indicator that they are going to be un-receptive to your request for part-time working.

Common challenge for a mum no. 4: Return to work support

As we've discussed, mums coming back from maternity leave don't seem to ask for return support because they don't know what to ask for. Most employers would admit that they are not experts in this area so the situation continues with both parties inwardly knowing those first few weeks could be better managed but not really making any progress.

Thankfully things are starting to change and employers are beginning to recognise that mums do need workplace support as they re-integrate. Maternity coaching for returning mums is becoming more commonplace within big companies and this is hopefully a sign of better things to come.

Rather than waiting for these measures to be adopted by your employer there are steps you can take to ensure you get the support you need in the first few weeks and months and we will cover these steps in Part 4 when we look at:

Recipe 2 – A Re-integration Support Proposal and

Recipe 3 – A Home Support Plan

Recap of a mum's perspective.

- However you are feeling about your return to work, you are not alone.

- Negative emotions are common. Try to understand what are causing yours and find a strategy that works for you.

- If you feel you have legal knowledge gaps don't worry, this book will help.

- By creating your own support plan for your workplace and your home you will enable your manager and your family to provide effective support as you ease back into work.

A manager's perspective

At the head office of Global Ltd, Paul is sat in his office contemplating his schedule. He has been valiantly juggling the demands of the modern business world with a depleted team since Anna left. He recruited a recent graduate as maternity cover for Anna's role. The young man started just as Anna left in September but within three months he had accepted a permanent job on a graduate training scheme elsewhere and he was gone by the end of December. Paul wasn't best pleased but he understood why a graduate would favour a permanent job with long term prospects over a short term contract covering maternity leave. At least the team had benefited from extra help through to financial year end. Paul is now producing many of the reports that Anna used to create and Tina, a more junior member of the team, is attending Anna's meetings as a deputy. It's a good development opportunity for Tina but Paul will be glad to have Anna back and hopefully it won't be long now!

Since Anna started her maternity leave in September there have been many changes. Global Ltd has introduced a market leading new product range (with initial quality problems) and discontinued an older product range (with higher than expected write off costs). A review by the Global IT harmonisation team has concluded that the UK head office will need to replace one of the core systems in the next 18 months in order to align with group operating policy. This means that very soon one member of Paul's team will need to be selected for secondment onto that project. It is not clear at this stage whether the new system will ultimately mean an organisational re-structure i.e. bring redundancies. To add to the pressure last month a long serving team member, David, surprised everyone by resigning to join a competitor. The remaining team members are trying to cover his work but the cracks are beginning to show. Juggling more than just his own responsibilities while recruiting means Paul is also working long hours. He doesn't have any spare time to plan ahead as he would like. Just doing the day-to-day work is a challenge.

Still, as he reflects, it's not been all hard work and no play at Global. As usual, the annual company conference was held in February and this year it was the best yet! The predictable New Year slump in morale was temporarily lifted as the head office team escaped en mass from the cold, gloomy British winter to sunny Barcelona for two days of presentations and workshops. It was wonderful! The change in climate along with the Mediterranean food and wine raised beleaguered spirits and helped to soften the blow as the board presented even more challenging targets for the new financial year.

Paul knows it is likely that Anna will be contacting him in the near future to discuss coming back to work. While he is delighted at the prospect of help on the horizon he is equally unsure what her commitment level will be. How will her new constraints reduce her ability to flex with the ever more demanding needs of the business? He has not managed an employee returning from maternity leave before and doesn't know how best to approach the situation. He hasn't received any advice or training on this topic and having looked on the company intranet is unaware of any internal re-integration policy for this scenario. As he scans his more recent unread emails he sees one from Anna asking to meet up for a chat. At this point Paul realises he is unprepared for her return. He doesn't know what his legal obligations are to Anna and what her rights are in coming back to the office. He starts making some hasty notes to take to HR.

- How long has Anna been on maternity leave?

- What's the name of her baby again?

- Is Anna entitled to her old job back? Is that the best place for her?

- What if Anna wants to come back part-time? What is the process and what do I need to do?

- Who on the management team has been through this already so I can pick their brains?

- How can I get her back up to speed quickly? Where is the new starter induction pack? That might be useful.

- I know it's important but where am I going to find the time to do all this?

As he turns back to the matters of the day his final thought about Anna makes his stomach lurch.

"My God! I hope she actually does want to come back! I don't need more recruitment!"

Four common challenges for a manager include:

1) Little awareness of flexible working legislation.
2) Lack of time and the absence of a re-integration policy
3) Using the company new starter induction.
4) Wondering how the returning mum will best rejoin the team.

Common challenge for a manager no. 1:
Little awareness of flexible working legislation

Does this sound familiar? In the same way that Anna feels under informed as she approaches this situation, Paul is also feeling a bit in the dark. For many managers the experience of childbirth within their own family is the only source of training they have had in this situation.

Most HR teams do usually have a maternity law expert and you probably know who that is in your company from speaking to them whilst pregnant. It's likely that this will be the person advising your manager about your flexible working application. At present in the UK it is not the norm to train managers in maternity law and flexible working legislation, although thankfully this is starting to change.

The obvious bottom line benefit for employers of training line managers in maternity law and flexible working rights is encouraging legal compliance and avoiding employment tribunals. The other benefits of training would include managers having increased confidence in managing you during your pregnancy, maternity leave and during your return to work. Surely that would be good for all concerned. Hopefully this will be the future reality that our daughters enjoy. Our reality today is rather different.

What does this mean for you?

Don't expect your manager to have the knowledge to guide you or answer your questions relating to your maternity rights or regarding your part-time working request. If they can't help it is probably because they are as much in the dark as you are, not because they want to make the experience more difficult for you.

Common challenge for a manager no. 2:
Lack of time and the absence of a re-integration policy

Paul's story was a snapshot of reality for many managers. The demands of their day-to-day role leave them little time to do anything other than their day job and designing a supportive return to work plan for you therefore doesn't easily get the top spot on their To Do list. However lack of time does not mean a lack of willingness to follow a procedure if one exists.

It's logical that the quality of your return to work experience is linked to the:

-   time and effort invested in planning it plus the
-   quality and relevance of the ideas within it and
-   genuine participation and support of your manager

It is not necessary that your manager builds your return plan. As we've already established, I strongly believe that, with the appropriate support, you are the best person to do that. In Paul's case he needs to use his limited time wisely and that would involve getting legal advice from the HR team and speaking to other managers who may have managed a return to work before. Provided that Anna has the specialist guidance that she needs, he can delegate the creation of Anna's re-induction plan to Anna. He can still have input into shaping it, help ensure that it is in place before Anna's return and that she stays on track during her return.

I am convinced that a re-integration policy that provides returning mums with the help they need to design their own personalised support programme would be most appreciated by mums and line managers alike. Managers would have guidelines to follow and apart from saving them time it would also help keep them on the legal straight and narrow and encourage a consistent return to work experience across even the largest business.

What does this mean for you?

If your company does not yet have a re-induction guide or procedure for your manager to follow, you can be proactive in asking him or her to champion your own personal return to work support programme. Your request will probably be sincerely welcomed because your manager will want things to go smoothly and well for you but won't have time to devote to it in the same way that you will.

Common challenge for a manager no. 3:
Using the company new starter induction

The temptation may be for Paul to re-induct Anna using the company's new starter induction, if there is one. Your employer may suggest that they do the same for you. While parts of it might be beneficial, such as last year's results and this year's targets, there are limitations and if it is used as the sole method of re-inducting you, it misses the mark for a number of reasons.

You probably already understand the workplace culture, the market, the product range and customer base. A successful re-induction plan needs to recognise your unique situation as you become (or return to being) a working mum. The business side of your re-induction needs to focus on what has changed while you have been away for example:

- Personnel changes so you have a chance to connect with people you may not have met before but with whom you will be expected to work
- System or procedural changes so you have opportunity to adjust to new ways of working
- Changes to the organisational structure or top management
- Current status of key projects that were underway or planned just before you left

Importantly the re-induction needs to include personalised support for the first few weeks and months including time to allow you to adjust to your new role as a working mum and time to get back up to speed as an employee. For these reasons a return support programme will look very different to a new starter induction.

What does this mean for you?

There are benefits to using the new starter induction and from your manager's perspective they may include:

- the pack already exists and is hopefully up to date so it saves time
- it is already accepted as a useful method for sharing important business information
- it re-immerses you in the company culture

The new starter induction has some benefits but also has limitations. If your manager offers you this you will be able to say "Thank you, yes please." and then ask him or her to consider other ways in which it can be expanded to more closely meet your needs. Having read this you will hopefully be better placed to explain the gaps that the new starter induction does not address and make some excellent proposals of your own to improve upon it.

Common challenge for a manager no. 4: Wondering how the returning mum will best rejoin the team

Paul wants Anna to rejoin the team and knows that she is entitled to return full time to her role or a similar role. Paul also recognises that she may not want to come back full-time. He appreciates she will add value back in the company but knows that part-time working, if it is requested, will need careful consideration. He may already have ideas about offering her the up-coming IT project role. He may be having thoughts about the pros and cons of re-shaping her current responsibilities. Whatever is in his head, he will first need to talk with Anna to understand on what basis she would like to come back to work. Key questions for Paul include:

- Does Anna want to apply for part-time working?

- If so what is she thinking of?

- Is she open to considering other roles?

- How flexible is she prepared to be?

- What are the implications for the team?

- Can the business accommodate it?

This type of open attitude to discussing a return to work does a business good. It encourages honest communication, thorough examination of the options and helps businesses retain talent. I encourage you to see your manager as being in this mindset because it will set you up well to have a positive conversation when you meet.

What does this mean for you?

Having walked a little in Paul's shoes you are better placed when you meet with your own manager to start to discuss your return. You can think about the sorts of questions he or she would find useful to have answers to. In fact, if your manager doesn't ask these questions, you can volunteer the information so they go away well informed.

Even if, at the time of the meeting, you are unsure about exactly what part-time working pattern or role you want to ask for you can re assure your manager that you want to remain open minded and flexible. You could ask useful questions such as:

- Who is currently doing the various elements of your job?
- How are they getting on?
- How has your role changed while you have been away?
- Where would you best slot back into the team?

Recap of a manager's perspective

- Like you, your manager has probably had no training in maternity law or flexible working legislation and if this is the case it will limit how much they can help you through the process. Don't worry, helping you through the process is what books like this one are for!

- Your manager is likely to be short of time and without any procedure to follow to support either of you when you go back to work. You can help both of you here with your Re-integration Support Proposal discussed in Part 4.

- If you are offered the new starter induction say "Yes please!" and use that as a way to start conversation about how it could form part of your support proposal.

- Your manager will be thinking about how best to slot you back into the team. He or she may have some ideas but they will not be able to develop them any further until you meet and talk. Re-assuring your manager that you are open-minded and flexible will help encourage more options to emerge for consideration.

A legal perspective

The two stories above highlighted that there is a general lack of legal awareness among mums and managers surrounding the return to work and the process for applying for part-time working. In order to plug key knowledge gaps this short section provides you with a plain English guide to the legal procedure governing flexible working applications. Extracts taken from the Employment Rights Acts 1996 are in a different font for clarity. For the sake of correctness I will revert to using the formal term 'flexible working request' in this legal section. By now you realise that there is a legal procedure associated with applying to work part-time but what does it cover exactly and what does that mean for you? The basics can be separated out as follows.

1. What is a flexible working request?
2. Who qualifies to apply?
3. How often can a flexible working request be made?
4. How do you make a flexible working request?
5. How should an employer consider and respond to a request?
6. The basic process and timelines
7. The possible outcomes

Let's look at each of these legal elements.

1. What is a flexible working request?

A flexible working request is made by an employee in order to allow them to care for a child or a dependent adult. It is a request to change their employment contract by altering the terms of the contract in one of three ways:

- Hours e.g. the overall hours in the contract of employment maybe reduced from 40 hours a week to 32 hours a week.
- Location e.g. working the same number of hours but working from home.

- Timing e.g. working the same number of hours in the same place but starting earlier and finishing earlier.

It is possible for a flexible working request to combine any of these three elements above. What is interesting is that many employers are using the return to work after maternity leave as an opportunity to offer mums entirely different roles as part of the new part-time working pattern. The Act does not mention change of role but it seems to be common practice and can work well for both parties. We will look at this in more detail in Part 2 in our interview with Helen.

2. Who qualifies to apply?

The qualifying criteria require that you must be a parent or carer with primary responsibility for the child and:

- have worked continuously for your employer for at least 26 weeks on the date of the application
- have not made a flexible working request in the last 12 months

The application can only be made to care for either

- a child under 17 years of age
- a disabled child under 18 years of age

The definition of parent is broad and includes

"either

- the mother, father, adopter, guardian, foster parent or a person who has been granted a residence order in respect of the child"

or a person who is

- married to or the partner of or civil partner of the mother, father, adopter, guardian, foster parent or a person who has been granted a residence order in respect of the child"

So as the mother of your baby, you qualify! Some forward thinking companies already operate a policy whereby any employee who has 26 weeks continuous employment can request flexible working.

3. How often can a flexible working request be made?

"An application can be made once in every rolling 12 months."

This covers any type of flexible working application request however so if you previously applied for flexible working to care for a dependant adult or for a different older child within the last 12 months then your employer could ask you to wait until a rolling 12 months have elapsed before allowing you to submit your next application in relation to your new baby. Employers are still people though and it would certainly be worth exploring the situation with them before assuming that they would make you wait.

4. How do you make a flexible working request?

The appropriate time to make your flexible working request is a few months before you would like to return to work. I would recommend you start the process three months before you actually want to return. This gives everyone involved enough time to consider your request or a workable alternative.

The UK Government website, www.gov.uk, provides a comprehensive guide to the flexible working application procedure for both employers and employees. Not only is the law explained for both parties but a series of template forms and letters are also available to provide additional support. You could use one of these template letters to start the process and make your application but do tailor your letter to make sure it has sufficient friendly overtones for your employer to warm to the content.

To comply with the formal process your application needs to be:

- Made in writing. Sending an email or a fax or posting a letter are all acceptable but applying via a phone call or a face to face meeting is not.

- Be clearly dated so that the process timings are clear to you and your employer.

- State that your application is "being made in accordance with your statutory rights".

- State that the application is being made in order to care for a qualifying child.

- Explain your relationship to the child so your employer can verify your eligibility to apply.

- Outline the new working pattern being requested.

- Indicate how you think this will impact on the business and make recommendations as to how your employer can reduce / remove any impact.

- Clarify the exact date that you would like the new working arrangement to start.

- For the benefit of your employer, make sure that if you have previously made an application for flexible working that you tell them when that was.

Do think about the impression your application will make on potential readers who may include your line manager and various HR colleagues. Obviously you will want to make sure you keep a copy of what you send for your own records. I look back with a mixture of horror and humour when I think about my own flexible working application. Despite not having a clue about the right way of doing things my letter was broadly in line with the legal requirements but, due to an imminent short holiday, I was in a hurry to write it and post it. My application was made via a scenic note-let depicting a view from the Lake District! My HR representative told me over the phone a few days later that it was the prettiest flexible working request the HR team had ever seen. She confided that many such applications came through hand written on a piece of A4 paper torn from a notebook complete with coffee stains and baby finger prints! It goes without saying that you want to make a good impression so a thoroughly spell checked printed letter or email would probably be a good idea and you probably want to avoid note-lets!

5. How should an employer consider and respond to your request?

As long as you meet the qualifying criteria you have the right to make a flexible working request but that does not mean that your employer is obliged to agree to it and implement your request.

Employers have an obligation to assess each application individually and their decision should reflect what is workable within the business rather than what they would personally prefer as a working arrangement.

An employer needs to be able to:

- demonstrate that they have given the request due thought and consideration.
- show that they have followed the process and timelines correctly.
- show that they have responded in writing in accordance with the legal guidelines.

That is all. As long as they have done the above then they have met their obligation. The next section comes from the website www.gov.uk

In rejecting a flexible working request employers must send a letter to the applicant outlining:

- the business reasons for rejecting the application
- an explanation about how flexible working affects their business
- how the employee can appeal

Employers can only reject an application for one of the following reasons:

- extra costs which would damage the business
- the business wouldn't be able to meet customer demand
- the work can't be re organised among other staff
- people couldn't be recruited to do the work
- flexible working would have an effect on quality and performance
- there's a lack of work to do during the proposed working times
- the business is planning changes to the workforce

If the employer doesn't agree to the request, they must have a meeting with the employee to discuss the reasons.

Thankfully most employers recognize the benefits of retaining quality and diversity of staff by accommodating their changing life situation, so please don't be disheartened by this section.

6. The basic process and timelines

Although there is a recommended letter template for you to use when you submit your request, most employers appreciate that employees are not legal professionals and an application that does not comply strictly with the requirements is unlikely to be rejected. Do be aware however that failure to comply with the application letter requirements could lead to rejection. You know your employer culture better than anyone so use your own judgment here. The template letter can be found and downloaded from www.gov. uk/flexible-working/making-a-statutory application

There is a strict and time bound procedure that your employer needs to follow once they have received your written request and you ought to be aware of this procedure too.

The table shows the basic flexible working application process

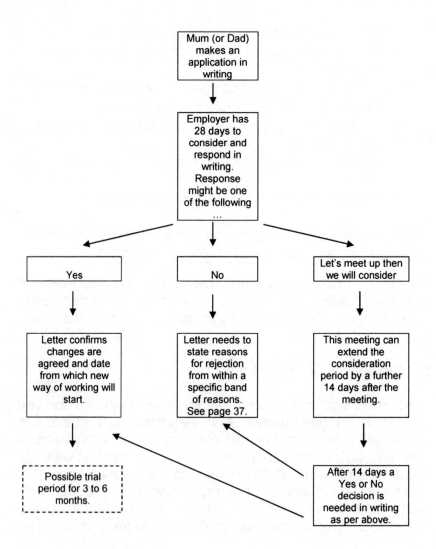

7. Possible outcomes

It boils down to a 'Yes' or a 'No' and company policy can vary considerably. In some companies there can be a blanket policy of deciding 'Yes' to flexible working requests from mums. In other companies each flexible working request is approved or rejected at the discretion of the individual line manager. There is no legal obligation for an employer to say 'Yes'.

It is because employers are not obliged to agree to your request that it can be a stressful time for you. As a parent it will be really important to you that you get a positive outcome and you will want to do the best job you can to persuade your employer to say 'Yes'. Designing a workable proposal and handling the negotiation effectively can feel like a big deal.

If you are reading this and recognize yourself then don't worry this is normal and is one of the fundamental ways in which this book is intended to help. At this point it might be a good idea to take a few deep breaths and remind yourself that you are already taking positive steps to achieving that end result.

The simple act of reading this legal section will help you to professionally approach your request and understand the process and your employer's obligations. It's a great place to be!

Please note that this legal section is correct as at the time of publication i.e. 2013. The Government has announced plans to change the legislation during 2014 or 2015. If you are interested in understanding more about the proposed changes then please refer to the Appendices at the back of this book.

Summary of Part 1

Part 1 set out to help you to look at the return to work from a variety of perspectives.

A mum's perspective

This section sought to reassure you that you are not alone in feeling apprehensive at the thought of going back to work. In looking at the experience through the eyes of another mum you saw the range of strong emotions that can collide during the build up to this life transition. You have been given some tools to help you to combat the more negative emotions of fear, guilt and dread. Hopefully knowing that this is all normal is a source of comfort and relief.

A manager's perspective

Looking at the return to work from a manager's perspective enabled you to start to reconnect with your own world of work and appreciate the challenges your manager may face during your transition. You are aware that you may need to be proactive with your manager because he or she is unlikely to have any support process or training to guide them. Having empathy for your manager and recognising the needs of the workplace will help enormously when you meet to discuss your return to work. Your increased awareness will add balance and objectivity to your thinking, attitude and behaviour.

A legal perspective

Finally, learning about the legal process behind flexible working legislation is fundamental as it enables you to move forward in a knowledgeable and self empowered way. You are now aware that there is a legal framework that sets out:

- How you can apply for part-time working in a technically complete manner.

- What your employers obligations are in considering your request.
- How your application should be processed.

Understanding the role that you need to play and also your employer's role enables you to feel prepared.

Let's now move on to Part 2 take a look at your options for part-time working.

PART 2

What are my part-time options?

Your options are endless!

There are many different categories of flexible working. The table below identifies some of the ways in which people can work flexibly.

Part-time working	Workers are contracted to work less than standard, basic, full-time hours.
Flexi-time	Workers have the freedom to work in any way they choose outside a set core of hours determined by the employer.
Staggered hours	Workers have different start, finish and break times, allowing a business to stay open longer.
Compressed hours	Workers can cover their standard working hours in fewer working days.
Job sharing	One full-time job is split between two workers.
Shift swapping	Workers arrange shifts among themselves, provided all required shifts are covered.
Self rostering	Workers nominate the shifts they would prefer, leaving the employer to compile the shift patterns matching individual preferences while covering all required shifts.
Term time working	A worker remains on a permanent contract but can take paid / unpaid leave during school holidays
Zero hours contract	Workers only work the hours they are needed.
Home working	Workers spend all or part of their week working from home or somewhere else away from the employer's premises.

Reading through this chart may have introduced you to options you had not previously considered or have given you ideas for new ways of working flexibly that are not listed above. There is no reason why different categories cannot be combined in your part-time working proposal making the number of scenarios available to you literally vast. For example you might ask to work Wednesday, Thursday and Friday (part-time) with Friday being a home based day (home working) spread over slightly different hours e.g. 8.00am till 4.30pm (staggered hours). This chart contains the basic ingredients for your part-time working request so you may want to fold back the edge of page 45 so that you can easily find it again later.

Three mums share their successful negotiation experience and part-time working pattern

We will shortly move on to three interviews with working mums who returned to work part-time after maternity leave. Clearly it is impossible to include examples of every type of part-time working pattern in a short book but each interview has been selected to provide you with variety. These interviews are deemed success stories not because the return to work was well supported and guilt free but because these women carefully designed and negotiated a part-time working pattern that met their needs, their employer's needs and the needs of their family. The only common theme to run through each account is utter honesty. No one has painted themselves as super woman. I am extremely grateful for their contributions. Providing you with insight into how their choices have worked in reality will serve to make your decisions better informed.

If we take a moment to go back to our cooking analogy, what these interviews show is how each woman has baked her own cake using different part-time ingredients that are appropriate for her, her particular family situation and her employer. Everyone's return to work is a different home-cooked recipe. Yours will be unique too. There is no right answer. You will know what the optimum combination is for you and your employer so please don't feel that you have to imitate others.

If you already have a good idea about what you want, that's great! The interviews will help you to think about the pros and cons of your chosen solution from both a work and home perspective before you actually try it for real. Now would be a good time to pick up your pen and write down what you are currently thinking of asking for and what you think the pros and cons will be for you, your family and your employer.

If you have no idea what you want to ask for, don't worry, that's normal. In fact, if all you know right now is what you don't want to do, then write that down and note the reasons why you don't want it.

As you read through the interviews I encourage you to jot down any ideas or insights that you find helpful or interesting and might like to investigate further. Try to group your thoughts into the following categories as identified by the Employment Rights Act.

- Change to Hours. For example, fewer overall contracted hours per week.
- Change to Timing. For example, start 1 hour early and finish 1 hour early.
- Change to Location. For example, home working vs office working.

- Change of Role. As mentioned before, a change of role is not mentioned in the Act as a flexible working option however a significant number of employers are using the return to work as an opportunity to offer mums different roles that might better fit a part-time working pattern. If this option sounds interesting to you then make some notes about the characteristics of a new role that might be workable e.g. moving to a:

  - project management role with clearly defined scope
  - specialist role with no direct reports
  - role with fewer relationships to maintain
  - role that does not require business travel

While watching television only last night I saw an interview with successful business woman Nicola Horlick. She explained that, while her children were very young, she held a demanding, high profile, full-time banking role but it was specifically focused on growing UK business on the behalf of UK clients. This removed the need for her to undertake foreign travel while her children were young. Changing the characteristics of a role does not mean creating a lesser role but it can make a big difference to the role's workability at this stage of your life.

There is no reason why a part-time role should equate to a diluted version of your previous job where a reduction in your responsibilities means that your career is treading water or stagnating. You are still an important member of the workforce with unique and valuable skills and you still require appropriate stretch, responsibility and recognition in order to thrive at work.

The job that you return to after maternity leave may be radically different to the one you had before maternity leave. It is of course for you to decide what type of role and what level of responsibility will work best for you and you should negotiate for that. If that is a stretching and demanding position that sets you up for the next promotion – go for it! Equally if that is a role that provides you with more gentle growth, perhaps in a new direction, then pursue that. You will read examples of each of these approaches in the interviews coming up with Helen and Suzy.

The bottom line is that part-time working does not make you less valuable, less effective or less influential in your workplace and a part-time role should not be a dead end for your career. Whatever role you return to after maternity leave, protection of your grade and salary are your legal entitlement. These elements cannot be changed without consultation and agreement between you and your employer. Obviously your take home salary will be subject to a pro rata reduction in line with your reduced hours and you will need to do the maths to make sure that this doesn't leave you struggling to make ends meet.

To help you to navigate the interviews, I've included a chart so you can easily compare how they differ. This will also help you to identify how the interviews may be similar to your own situation.

Table of Interviews

Name	Role	Company	Aspects changed in return to work	Details of interview	Duration of maternity leave
Julie	HR Manager	Motorsport organisation	Hours	Julie used accrued holiday to trial her old job on a 4 day per week basis before requesting part-time working.	6 months
Helen	Customer Service Manager	Global drinks manufacturer	Hours Role	Helen took a new project based role that gave her gentle growth and better fit part-time hours.	6 months
Suzy	Police Officer	Police force	Hours Timing Location Role	Suzy continued to pursue promotion and requested a new role in a new location on late shifts.	5 months

At the end of every interview each of the contributing mums will share any pearls of wisdom she feels that you, as a soon-to-be working mum, would benefit from. Finally I will identify the key points from the interview that I think are worth noting and understanding in more depth.

Introduction to Julie, HR Manager

Julie worked as the HR Manager at a motorsport organisation when her son was born. By that time Julie had been with the company for approximately 5 years. Julie returned to work when her son was 6 months old. The transition back to the office was eased significantly in the first few months as Julie's mother came to stay from Monday night to Friday night in order to provide childcare. This enabled Julie to focus on re-learning her role at work without simultaneously learning a new working mum routine. During this time Julie used an interesting and gentle approach to successfully persuade her employer that she could continue in her HR Manager role working 4 days a week.

Where was your career at the point at which you started your maternity leave?

I was employed as an HR Manager with three people working for me. I worked full-time and technically I was contracted to work 40 hours a week but, as is the case with many people, it was often more than 40 hours a week. I'd go in early, leave late and maybe have half an hour for lunch or no lunch. That's the nature of the world today I think. You have standards of performance that you want to meet and you work the hours required to deliver that. Pre children you can do that because you just stay later. You never have a clear in-tray but you get it to the point where you are comfortable.

How old was your baby when you went back to work?

He was 6 months.

What were your reasons for going back at that point?

Well, obviously finances came into the decision. They certainly did for me. I wasn't in the position where I could choose not to work but it was also about a sense of self and that was important for me. It wasn't that I felt the need to further my career or get to the next step of being HR Director in a multi-national company. For me it was important to do a good job and have a sense of self esteem beyond being a mum. I think that for some people being a dedicated mum is enough and that's fine but it wasn't going to be that way for me.

When did you actually start to plan your return to work?

When I left for maternity leave I already had a good idea that I'd want to go back to work once my baby was 6 or 7 months old. Before I left work I told my employer that November was when I planned to return, which I did.

What did you decide to do for childcare?

Well, I left arranging childcare until quite late but I knew I wanted a childminder rather than a nursery. Obviously that's an individual choice for each family and they need to choose what suits them. Even before he was born I wanted him to be with a childminder rather than a nursery but I hadn't done anything about identifying a childminder or reserving a place. I kind of had this ridiculous blind faith that it would work out, which it did. I was fortunate though because my mum had agreed that she would come and help in the first few months. Bless her! She came and lived with us for 4 nights a week and that eased the initial return to work because in those first few months I didn't need to get baby out of the house and me out of the house. I could leave him with my mum which felt very different to leaving him with paid help.

That sounds like excellent support to have when you go back to work.

Absolutely and because she was Granny I wasn't embarrassed by the fact that I might call her three times a day or that I wanted to know every little bit of detail of my baby's day.

I'm guessing it worked because you get on well with your mum!

Yes I was lucky that she was happy to do it and that my father was happy for her to do it and that my husband was happy for her to be here. My husband and I really value 'our time' once baby has gone to bed so obviously it was important that we all got on. It really did make that transition so much easier to have her there. I didn't have that mad rush in the morning to get up and get out on time and get my child dressed and breakfasted as well. It also meant that if I was 10 minutes late leaving the office or the traffic was bad on my way home I didn't have to worry that I was going to be fined for being late. I could just ring her and let her know I was on my way, running a bit late and ask if everything was ok.

Did you stay in touch with your manager during your maternity leave?

Yes. During the time I was off I had a few meetings with my line manager, usually in the evenings either at the office or in the pub. We'd discuss things like:

- How I might use Keep In Touch days
- What was going on in the office
- My return plan and what I was thinking of doing

It was following these discussions that I wrote formally to the company requesting their agreement for my return to work on the basis that I worked full-time but used my accrued holiday from my maternity leave to effectively be in the office 4 days a week. This meant that from the November, when I went back, to the following February I was testing how workable a part-time working pattern might be.

My intention was always that I would use that time to prove to them and to me that I could perform in my role on a four day a week basis. After I'd done that for a while I approached them with a formal request for flexible working and that's how it eventually got agreed. From then on I officially worked 4 days a week and I still do now.

That's a really interesting approach to requesting flexible working. Most mums apply before the end of their maternity leave but you applied after you'd been back a few months. It clearly worked for you and your company! Does working 4 days a week give you the right kind of work / family balance?

Yes, I think it does most of the time. I still work a 32 hour week, which is a lot for part-time work, and I sometimes think that in an ideal world I'd prefer to work 3 days a week. In reality it can be a stretch to do all that I need to do in 4 days a week so I don't know how 3 days would work. Maybe if I worked 3 days a week that would mean that I'd be considered to be more 'part-time' and therefore the expectations of me at work would be lower. I'm not convinced.

From where I am in my position I see a lot of what goes on and I actually think that you can get much more out of two motivated part-time employees than you can out of one full-time employee.

Yes, in my experience, mums who work part-time tend to want to get to work and give it their all being as efficient and effective as possible until they have to leave.

Yes, I agree with you completely, you are just more focused. Your whole approach is "I need to get this done because I need to leave on time." It would be lovely to have a chat over a cup of coffee about this or that and previously you would have done exactly that and stayed later to get things finished but now you no longer have that option. I think also that during your maternity leave you have juggled so many different priorities, so in some ways you have a different and more developed skill set as well.

It makes a nice change to go back to work and use that skill set and find you can get things done in a normal amount of time.

Yes! Another thing that was great about going back to work was managing to finish a whole meal uninterrupted! And have a conversation. We have a rule at work that you cannot eat at your desk. You have to go to the restaurant on site. You can eat your own food or buy it. But just to sit and eat something that doesn't go cold half way through or you didn't have to get up in the middle of or you weren't trying to eat one handed. Where you could use a knife and a fork, all of those things were a revelation.

It's just the simple things in life like drinking an entire cup of tea while it's still hot!

Yes! And it sounds so silly doesn't it to someone who hasn't been there. I do think that's one of the small rewards even though it may only be half an hour, it's still half an hour for me!

If I can take you back to those days and weeks when you did go back to work can you describe what it was actually like to go through that change process?

Even though I had help at home and I had faith in the childcare I'd put in place it was really hard in reality.

I think you leave a role at a certain level of expertise and performance both in terms of how you perceive yourself but also, rightly or wrongly, how you perceive other people think about you. So when I left I'd been with the business 5 or 6 years. I had seen things change and grow and evolve. I knew what was going on, where things were at, not just the major structural changes that people can tell you about and that you can catch up on but also the subtle politics and fallings out etc. When you walk back into work, you walk into that void because you haven't been there for over 6 months. So I felt out of control actually not knowing what had happened or what sort of mine field I was walking into.

I had the same expectations of myself when I went back as I'd had before I left and that was unrealistic. Previously I'd often had to work late, as I've described, but that was no longer an option. I think I put pressure on myself and I did feel bad that I left on time and that I was leaving my team in the office on many occasions. I think you lead by example and I'd never ask my team to do something I wasn't prepared to do myself.

I also felt that others expected me to be on the ball with it all, just as I had been before I left. At the point of my return I just didn't know what had gone on in my absence. I had to remind people that I hadn't been there "So fill me in". I think the 6 months had flown for them so they had almost forgotten that I hadn't been there and been out of the loop. I just felt a bit at sea if I'm honest with you.

What other challenges did you face as you returned to work?

Well, during that time I also had a fear that my job had been done better by the person covering my maternity leave. In reality it was a bit ridiculous because it was my job but that didn't change the way I felt.

You are definitely not alone with that one. That's a common little niggling worry that most of us have. It's completely normal.

But I don't think people talk about it on the whole. It is quite difficult to admit that in your workplace or to your line manager because it sounds like you are insecure or not good enough at your job that you think that someone else could do it better than you. Thoughts go round your head such as:

> "They might be doing a better job than I did."
> "The team might like them more than me."
> "The company might want that person to do the role instead of me."
> "The company won't want me back working flexibly. They will only want me back on the same full-time basis as before."

All these things are, on the whole, largely unfounded.

One thing that you mentioned just now was that your expectations of yourself were the same as when you had left and that you recognised that this was unrealistic.

I think it took a while for me to recognise that it was unrealistic and that was part of my re-adjustment period. If I am perfectly honest, I still struggle sometimes.

On the one hand I am leading by example by doing my job in the hours I'm paid for but when there is a push on and something has to be sent out to all employees and everyone in my team is there stuffing envelopes or making sure the right paperwork is going out – that's the time when it is really hard to get up and walk away. When I mentioned my discomfort with that situation my team told me:

"Well don't feel bad because you shouldn't. It's about how well you do your job not about when you are leaving or whether you are leaving on time."

I've come to the conclusion that when it's unrealistic and I can't do something I won't feel bad about it.

The other thing I found was difficult in the first few months, but that has changed with time, is that people would call meetings in the afternoon or maybe half an hour before I was due to leave. Previously I would have stayed until the meeting had finished but to actually get up in a meeting, largely full of men at a senior level, and say;

"I have to go now."

takes an awful lot of courage and makes you feel very small.

It makes you feel self conscious?

Yes, and it's frustrating because I feel that I want to have an input into this meeting and the outcome of it and if I'm not here I can't influence it.

Have you been able to influence when meetings are held now?

Yes. It was my learning curve and also that of my colleagues. It was part of setting expectations at the beginning. I found myself saying to people

"If we need to meet at that time then ok we need to meet at that time but you've only told me about that today and I can't make alternative arrangements. You need to know that I've only got half an hour and I need to leave at a certain time to collect my son."

I think that people have learned to give me more notice because actually I can juggle things slightly or ask my husband to pick my child up or ask the childminder for another half an hour or juggle my day somehow if I'm given enough warning. But I can't do it at the drop of a hat. And it's the law according to sod isn't it that you can bet an emergency happens when your husband is away!

Have you had any experience of child sickness and juggling work in that circumstance?

The first night I did a night away with work, which was a course I was involved in running, my little boy was very ill. It wasn't life threatening but it was serious to the point that my childminder contacted my office and my husband to say that he needed collecting. He had a temperature and she had other little ones to look after. He needed to be at home. I can't really remember what it was but I did have to take my son to the GP and again I remember thinking "Ok, so now what?" I've never really gotten used to that. Work related stuff I can cope with but child sickness is really tricky. Obviously if my son is unwell he usually wants me, his mother, but on the flip side is the fact that I've planned to interview someone or attend a meeting that day. I can't do these things now and I can't leave my son unwell. I think there's an element of balance that is quite difficult about that.

I think you raise a really valid point there. Child sickness is inevitable and it can be the cause of additional stress for a working mum if she doesn't know how her manager wants her to handle it. Discussing it up front is helpful for everyone. If you share a common understanding with your line manager on this topic then you are not worrying about your child's health and also worrying about letting work down or mishandling the situation.

That's true and I think in fairness we probably don't do that in my company right now. I think there is a general expectation that you would take a days leave and if you are lucky maybe your husband or partner can share the childcare and you can do a half day each. But again that depends upon the child and how ill they are and how much they want their mummy.

Did you make any tweaks to your working pattern once you were back?

Yes, one small change made a big difference. I agreed with my husband that he will pick my little boy up on a Friday night which means I can stay late on a Friday and just get things to a point where I am happy to leave it till Tuesday morning. This means I can relax over the weekend. That really helps in terms of me feeling satisfied. I'm not thinking over the weekend or during Monday "Gosh, I didn't do this" or "I've got that to finish." That's not to say that there haven't been occasions when I've been in the office during a weekend and done a few bits or even on a Monday for a half day but that has been pre planned and pre organised.

That sounds really helpful! So your part-time working arrangement is one that you thought carefully about, worked with and made changes to. How do you know you've got the right work / family balance?

There isn't a simple answer to that because I think you always want more balance. There are still things that challenge me and make me feel guilty that I'm not there for my child or not there for the business. If I could give advice to a new mum it would be about recognising that you are human and that you can only do what you can do. Try and get a balance that works for you and that you can live with. It's not perfect.

It's always a compromise?

Yes, on the whole what I've got works and I'm really lucky in that I have excellent childcare and that makes such a big difference. It's finely balanced though and it only takes one unexpected event to throw me off balance. The most disruptive events for me are child sickness or a crisis at work. I am fortunate though because I know my childcare provider would be ok with me arriving a little late if something happened at work. My husband and I try to share how we handle child sickness so it's not always me taking time off.

Julie, thank you for your time today! I have just one more question. In order to help our soon-to-be working mums, what would you say were the things that made you certain that your return to work was gradually getting easier?

It's difficult to say really. It is something that I have become more comfortable with over time, though there are still days when it is difficult even now. But it is like most things, you get used to it with time and make the adjustments required and even enjoy it! It was probably months rather than weeks before it felt normal and easier.

Do you remember any specific signposts that gave you encouragement?

It was a mixture of things both at home and at work that made it feel easier:

- At home my son and I got into a routine and with practice, as it became familiar; it became quicker to accomplish the same thing.
- I decided to stop beating myself up about my home being untidy. I'm not going to have written on my gravestone;

"I wish I'd done more housework!"

Within minutes of tidying everything up the place looks messy again anyway.
- It took a while for me to work out some relatively simple things that made a big difference. For me it was my husband doing the collection on a Friday so I could stay a little later and get my work into an order that I was happy to return to the following Tuesday. It gave me headspace then over the weekend without having to worry about what I hadn't completed and also enabled me to deliver on things I had to get done by the end of the week.
- Work wise the more time you are back the more you are in the picture with what is going on, therefore the more confident you are in your contribution, opinions and decision making. Feeling back in control of what was going on was really important to me and that took time.
- Positive feedback is great and once you hear you are doing a good job, a weight is lifted off your shoulders.
- The final factor for me was when my colleagues began to realise that I no longer work on Mondays and started to plan around that. When I stopped having to repeat it one hundred times a week I felt a lot better. It was evidence that the organisation was adapting to my new way of working and that was really helpful.

Key Points from Julie's interview

1) Be aware of the common re-integration challenges

The work-based challenges that Julie mentions on the return to work are quite normal in the first few weeks and months:

- Initial feelings of being out of control, out of the loop, basically outside of what's going on.
- Self doubt and comparison to the person who covered the maternity leave.

- Unrealistic expectations about overtime and the necessary adjustment to new time constraints with associated guilt.
- Colleagues taking time to learn to accommodate her new part-time working pattern.
- Challenges posed by child sickness, both from a company and personal perspective.
- Leaving meetings before they have ended to collect baby and feeling self conscious and disadvantaged.

The home-based re-integration challenges were reduced for Julie but were still present in the form of:

- Needing to find childcare quite close to her return date.
- Sadness at her reduced one-to-one time with baby.
- Self criticism about having a messy home.

Given that these challenges, self doubts and worries were simultaneous it is no wonder that it took a few months to feel as though things were getting easier! It is highly likely that you will encounter some, if not all, of these challenges yourself at some point in the first few months. During this time it is really important that you are kind to yourself but also honest. There may be aspects of your new routine that are working well and which would be good to identify and others that are not working as well as you'd hoped and need a re-think.

2) Keep in touch with your manager

Julie's interview highlights the importance of staying in touch with your employer during maternity leave and how this can help the subsequent negotiation of your part-time working pattern. The gradual move to formalising her 4 day week enabled both Julie and the management team to see that it would work in practice. Her successful negotiation was the result of collaboration with her line manager who understood the company culture and shared Julie's desire to see a win-win outcome.

3) Characteristics of engaged part-time working mums

These have been mentioned in Julie's interview and are well worth pulling out again so you can refer to them if you need to. Part-time working mums generally:

- Work as productively as possible whilst at work
- Manage their time carefully
- Prioritise effectively
- Respect the time of others
- Stay focused on delivery

4) Acknowledge your re-integration landmarks

Signposts for Julie that helped her to see her return was getting easier were:

- The morning routine bedding in for both her and her baby
- Realising that a small change can bring a big benefit e.g. working later every Friday to get things to a reasonable state before the weekend plus Julie's husband agreeing to pick the baby up that night so that this was possible.
- Colleagues learning that she now works 4 days a week.
- Positive feedback at work to let her know she was doing a great job.

These moments or others like them will be re-integration landmarks for you too so do look out for them and congratulate yourself privately along the way. A key moment for me was sitting in a meeting and making a valuable and insightful contribution, as if I'd never been away. I remember thinking to myself at the time, "Wow! Did I just say that?"

5) Practice pragmatism

Julie has a very pragmatic approach to being a working mum and mentions a number of realities that all working mums find themselves wrestling with.

- Her work / family balance is fragile and the whole thing can be knocked off balance by just one unexpected variation from the norm e.g. a meeting that over runs or child sickness. With experience, you do learn to handle these events well. Don't worry if the first few attempts are difficult to navigate. Discussing late collection flexibility with your childcare provider and a child sickness procedure with your line manager will help.

- She sometimes wonders whether she has got the balance right and whether working three days a week would be better. Regardless of whether women go back to work full or part-time, they still find themselves analysing whether they are doing the right thing for themselves, their career, their baby, their family, their employer. Basically, if you are happy most of the time then it's probably right for everyone.

- Julie recognises that some days are easier than others and that is still the case now. The return to work gets easier over time but being a working mum is a constant juggling act. While you may never feel masterful you will definitely get better at keeping all your plates spinning with practice.

<u>Where is Julie now?</u>

Julie has been promoted to the new role of Head of HR at the same motorsport organisation under the same 4 day part-time working pattern.

Introduction to Helen, Customer Service Manager

Helen worked as a Customer Service Manager during her first pregnancy. Helen's interview contains an interesting assessment of part-time working dynamics and explores the benefits of returning to work on a part-time basis to a totally different role.

Where was your career at the point at which you left on maternity leave?

My career was in a decent place. I was reporting to a board member. It's difficult to know exactly how people rate you but I would say that I was reasonably well regarded in the role I was doing. If I had not stopped to have children I would like to think that 5 years would have put me onto board level. Interestingly, although that was all fine, I was beginning to feel as though corporate life wasn't for me. I felt a bit jaded, as though I spent my life making shareholders richer and I was applying myself to that when I could be applying myself elsewhere and have greater self worth.

I suppose to onlookers my career was in a good place and I was successful in my role.

Did that mean working long hours?

Yes, the kind of hours that a professional role requires. No one expected me to work long hours but it was probably at least 6.30pm and often later than that before I left in the evening. But I didn't mind. It wasn't forced upon me. I was doing those hours because I wanted to do a decent job. I'd start sometime around 8.00am to 8.30am but then I'd spend a reasonable amount of time during the day talking and drinking coffee as well so I'm not sure I was particularly effective in that time. I'm much more effective with my time now. Prior to having children I'd work much longer hours but my typical day would include more sitting around drinking coffee and complaining about life!

That's very honest! Noah was your first child. How old was he when you went back to work?

Noah was 6 months old but going back to work then was a mistake. I didn't really mean for that to happen. At 6 months my boss and I were having a call and I think I had already decided that I wouldn't go back full-time. At that point there was no one in the business working 3 days a week and although I wasn't trying to hold my manager to ransom I did say that I would only go back to work on 3 days a week. I actually thought the business would say 'No', but he said;

"Yes, the Customer Service Manager role is already covered and it needs full time focus but there is a Supply Chain Development role available that could be done on a part-time basis. Ok, yes, I'll have you back on 3 days."

It felt a bit like a double bluff and then I panicked and thought well I might as well give it a go because if it didn't work out I could always stop. So I went back to work after 6 months, which was earlier than I'd intended, but only because the opportunity was there to work 3 days a week. If he'd said 'No' to me working 3 days a week then I don't know what would have happened.

Different path?

Yes

What were your reasons for going back to work?

I think I went back to work to retain my independence, my mental, physical and financial independence.

Was your return to work something that you thought about much?

No, no I decided not to think about it. My mum is brilliant. She so practical and level headed and I take lots of advice from her. In the first weeks after Noah was born she'd said;

"Don't try to organise anything. Don't worry about anything, don't try and get into a routine. Just go with it."

I think she and I discussed my return to work quite soon after the birth at around August time and she said;

"Don't even think about going back to work till after Christmas."

So I don't think I did. I had no plan. I don't think you can have a plan too early on. I think it's very difficult if you try to be organised and have a plan from the start.

So you took your mum's advice and waited until after Christmas?

Yeah, it was in the January that I had the phone call with my boss and I went back in the February part-time. I ended up writing my own job description. They said I needed to be clear on what I would do in those 3 days.

That sounds positive. Did it give you the opportunity to decide how broad your job description was going to be so you could make sure you didn't over commit yourself to delivering more than was realistic?

Yes

When you were deciding how many days you wanted to work each week, was that decision influenced by your mum?

Yes, in terms of the number of days definitely. Working 3 days a week means you spend more time away from work than in work and it just feels like a good balance. When you're in work it gives you enough to get your teeth into but because you are only there 3 days you aren't treated as though you can somehow miraculously do the same volume of work as a full-time employee. You can still make a difference and you can still influence but, in my opinion, you're never going to have the expectations put on you that you do if you work reduced hours Monday to Friday or if you work a four day week. I really do think that it is easy to become overloaded if you work more than 3 days a week. I think 3 days is a tipping point for manager expectations in terms of volume of work.

Very interesting! There may be some truth in that. Did your request to work 3 days a week take much negotiation with your manager?

It was an open conversation. I was fortunate that he had recruited me in the first place. He'd taken a risk on moving me from the Sales team, where I'd been a National Account Manager, into the Customer Service role in his Supply Chain team. He had liked what I had done in the 6 months that I was in that role. It definitely helped me because what he had 'bought' in recruiting me was a link into Sales department that the Supply Chain department hadn't had previously. I think he wanted to keep that. So I think there is a piece about the relationship you have with your line manager.

The other thing is, when you come back, you can't dictate to your manager what you are going to do. It has to be soft and gentle for example:

"I'm proposing that I come back initially on 2 days a week and then build up to 3 days a week".

Because I think you can frighten employers by being forceful. It's all about the positioning and how you negotiate.

Yes, I think that's true but having a clear idea of what you want helps your employer to decide. You explained to your manager that you wanted to work 3 days a week but you were open to what the role might look like. Was the role you were offered the same grade as your previous role?

Yes same grade, same everything. In fact that development role was a really great job. It was a national decline in market demand for our product that ultimately meant the role and other roles were not sustainable. I'm confident that due to having me back working 3 days a week there became more of us doing that. Every employee had to reapply for their job in the redundancy situation that came later on and I'm confident that I could have retained the same grade but I would probably have had to go back to working 4 days a week. In the end I took redundancy but my leaving wasn't to do with my performance or my being a working mum.

What were your hours / days when you returned to work after having Noah?

I worked 3 days a week from 9.00am to 5.30pm on Tuesday, Wednesday and Thursday. Interestingly I'm now back working with the same corporate group in a sister company and I work the same hours but on a Monday, Wednesday and Thursday instead and I feel more connected with the business.

Yes, Monday can be a key operational day that gets you on the same page as everyone else and sets you up for the rest of the week.

Yes. I think if you are doing a project role then it matters less what days you work but if your role is in the slightest way related to the day to day running of the business then you need to be in on a Monday.

Otherwise you have your Monday on Tuesday when everyone else has moved on.

Yes, exactly! Three days together is too long but you need to have two days together to get any kind of rhythm to your work and feel like you are making progress.

And that is something you've come to acknowledge since you've changed to working Monday, Wednesday and Thursday?

Yes, the weird thing about working Tuesday, Wednesday and Thursday was that it was like doing the old Monday to Friday but out of sync with everyone else. I'd get in on Tuesday and it was "Go!" I couldn't ease myself in and say to people "Did you have a good weekend?" because it had been and gone. Likewise on Thursday, as I left, I couldn't say "Have a good weekend!" because it was still a working day away.

So actually going back to work when Noah was 6 months old, what were the first few weeks like in your new role?

As an employee it was good. It was exciting to be back. It was a luxury to not be thinking about anyone else apart from myself and I think I enjoyed being at work again. I had been slightly disillusioned before my pregnancy about corporate life but suddenly I found a new vigour for work because I was choosing to be there. It was in second place behind my family life and I really enjoyed that. I liked the vibe, liked the energy and liked being back. I didn't have any guilt about putting Noah into nursery. I felt comfortable about that. He was physically close to me because he was less than a mile away from the office and that weirdly gave me some kind of comfort. I think I actually felt relief on some mornings! The strange thing was that after I had gotten past lunch I arrived at a point in the afternoon when previously I would have dipped (I don't dip now I work part-time – I don't have time!) but at that point, about 2.30pm to 3.30pm, I'd think;

"I've had enough now. I want to see my baby."

I just wanted to give him a cuddle. I probably had that feeling for quite a long time. Then at 5.30pm I would go and get him and go home and I would be absolutely exhausted! Doing a full working day, especially with my husband being away on business a lot at that point, coming home and doing the feed, bath, milk, bed, I was exhausted! It would take me all my time to get back downstairs, feed myself something and then I'd just fall asleep on the sofa!

But it was only like that until I got into the rhythm of it. Then it was fine. I do much more now because I'm shipping two young boys around and I'm perfectly capable of going out in the evenings but in those first few months I was exhausted by 7.30pm! That was it! Lights out! Go to bed!

I can relate to that very well.

I suppose going back to work was good. I missed Noah in the afternoons and the whole thing was physically exhausting. I just wonder what I was doing in the mornings before I had my children. I could get up, shower and choose which outfit to wear but now it's so full on. Getting myself up and getting dressed and getting them up and giving them breakfast.

And changing a soiled nappy just as you are on your way out the door!

Yes, really busy isn't it?

What sort of support did you get when you went back to work first of all?

I don't recall anything different happening that reflected the fact that I was coming back to work. I don't recall having any conversations specifically relating to the fact that I'd had a baby.

So the fact that you were pleased to be back and you re-integrated well and you enjoyed your new role, wrote your own job description and found it a good experience was entirely down to you and your disposition rather than anything else?

Yes, there was no support from work about how I was coping. I was sort of all on my own and talking to other people and other friends who'd been there.

Did you have some kind of network outside of work that gave you some support?

No, the people who supported me informally were in work, about three of them.

Well that's good. Did you therefore get the work / family balance from working 3 days that you were looking for?

Yes, I think that working part-time is great for mental health generally because while you are in work you apply yourself consistently, effectively and sensibly. I think you are less likely to get involved in politics. I think you possibly become a more valuable employee to a business because you'll just do more. You are more effective with your time and also you probably put a lid (well I certainly did, rightly or wrongly) on immediate future aspirations. I just got on with doing the very best job I could in the job I was doing.

And, to an extent, being grateful for having the opportunity to do that part-time?

Yes, I think so! In fact in doing all these things it's like a virtuous cycle. You apply yourself more, do more, deliver more, feel better and feel more empowered. It all kind of cycles well and I wish I could have explained that to my 25 year old self but of course the world doesn't work that way. It gives me the balance that I wanted because it doesn't consume me.

I think the nice thing is that regardless of what problems have gone on in the office you can't and you don't want to carry that home with you. To be honest it all just melts away the minute that little person grins at you anyway. It just falls out of your head. By the time you've gotten home and given them a bath and read stories and sung to them it kind of does the same thing as going to the gym used to do. Work angst is just gone. So you don't dwell on it. It doesn't become an issue. You can go back into work fresh the next day.

You find it gives you separation and perspective?

I think it does but even if I hadn't gone back to work in the corporate world I think I would have always tried to find something to do with my time to keep me away from my kids for a period of time in the week. I think it's good for me to have the break. If you create a balance that means you are happy and they are happy then you're not going to be booking time on the psychiatrists couch! You just have to go with what feels right for you.

And you'll know what feels right and what doesn't?

If it feels right for you then your kids will take their cue from you. If it feels right and you don't have any guilt and it's not stressing you out and not making you feel upset then the chances are it's not making them feel upset either.

Is there anything you would do differently with hindsight? Do more or do less?

I don't think so but then I was really fortunate when I went back to my company initially. I'm glad I had clarity in my own head about wanting to work 3 days a week and no more. I think it's important to know what your cut off point is in negotiating with your employer. Everything is up for debate in the future but at this time in your life you need to know what your 'best and final' position is. I'm really glad that I had my 3 day stance and I'm still doing it a number of years later because it's still the right balance while my boys are small. Some mornings, when I'm trying to drag my boys out of the door to nursery, I just remind myself that this is fine because tomorrow morning we can sit round in our pyjamas and play. I feel very lucky.

You've already provided lots of food for thought and plenty of advice but is there anything else you think a new mum going back to work should bear in mind?

I think we are all the same when it comes to our kids. We all want the best for them. I think you can work and still spend a sensible amount of time with your kids but you have to be happy about it not to feel any guilt about it. That would be my advice. Do what you have to do to support your family and do what you want to do to keep you happy and then just get on with it. Make sure that the time you do spend with your kids you then enjoy and value.

Key points from Helen's interview

1) Ask for what you want

A significant factor in Helen's successful return to work was her clarity that she wanted to work 3 days a week and no more. While she didn't "hold her manager to ransom", she was clear on this point when discussing her return to work with her boss. In her own mind she was quite prepared not go back at all if her boss could not accommodate this part of her request. Being clear about what you definitely do not want is just as valuable as knowing what you do want.

Wherever you have clarity about your desired working pattern, make a note of it.

2) Stay open minded to new opportunities

Helen was open minded to taking a different role upon her return to work and saw the change to a project based role as a real opportunity to scope out a manageable job. Moving away from an operational role into a process improvement role was very appealing to Helen. It removed the stress of day-to-day operational responsibility. It meant no longer having direct reports. It allowed Helen to focus all her attention on delivering improvement at a pace that she could influence and also enabled her to write her own job description and decide what was in scope for her role.

3) Give proper consideration to the part-time working dynamic you request

Helen mentioned giving careful thought to the days she selected to work part-time. Working part-time really does create a different dynamic and if you have only ever worked full-time prior to having your baby you might find that a surprise. This is something that is worth discussing with your employer as you assess what might be the most appropriate working pattern for the job and the team that you will be part of.

- What are the busiest days of the week for the team?
- Do you need to attend any key meetings during the week and if so on what days?
- Who do you need to work closely with?
- Do they work part-time?
- How will your chosen working pattern affect your ability to manage and maintain key relationships?

All these questions and others can help you to arrive at a practical workable solution.

4) Get yourself support

Just as in the previous interview with Julie, Helen relied upon her mum for valuable support during her maternity leave. Helen's mum had also gone back to work after Helen was born and could appreciate Helen's situation. It is always useful to draw upon your network of family and friends for help and advice but this is one situation where you will need to be selective. Choose the advice that works for you and disregard the advice that doesn't, regardless of who it has come from. If you are unable to draw upon your mum for support and advice in this situation remember that you are not alone. Sometimes close friends and relatives just cannot understand the desire / need to go back to work. It is important that you find people who will support you and build you up during this transitional phase. There may be working mums at your office that you can contact and chat to or women at your baby group who have just gone back to work. Whatever you do – don't go it alone!

5) That happy working mum feeling

Helen talks about feeling 'comfortable' with the 3 day working pattern she has and the positive impact that being a happy working mum has on her, her family and her workplace. Knowing what is right for you is something only you will be able to define and you may discover what works through trial and error. Helen's example shows that when you have got it right, you feel it. Life is not always a bed of roses, but in the main, when your working pattern fits your life situation, you find you can generally meet expectations on all sides.

Where is Helen now?

Helen is still employed by the same company on the same working pattern but in a different project focused role.

Introduction to Suzy, Police Officer

Suzy joined the police force after graduating. She is married to Ian and they have two children. Before her first pregnancy Suzy applied for promotion to sergeant. She discovered she was pregnant in the middle of the promotion assessment process.

Where was your career when you started maternity leave?

I'd been a police officer for 8 years since graduating. My first 3 years had been in front line policing i.e. uniform but for the next 5 years I'd been working in the domestic violence unit in my area. By that point I was pretty much running the unit so I knew I was ready to go for promotion.

In order to pass my sergeant exams I had offered to go back to front line policing. In the police this is a normal part of the promotion process if you have been out of uniform for some time. This meant a change of location for me. It meant I was working nearer to home which reduced my commute considerably. So I'd just sat my part 1 sergeant exam when I discovered I was pregnant and I was due to sit my part 2 exam when I started my maternity leave so obviously that exam had to be delayed until I came back.

How was your pregnancy accommodated in your role?

I was fortunate to have a manager who had children of his own so when I told him I was pregnant he put me on nice hours Monday to Friday 9.00am till 4.00pm. At that time, although I still had to pass my formal exams, I was doing a sergeant role as active duty, but this was fine because I didn't have to respond. That means I didn't have to go out to jobs, it was all office based. I was meeting the public and witnesses but I didn't have to deal with offenders. For me, at that time, that was great! In addition, because I was doing an active sergeant role – I also got a pay rise too!

So your manager took positive steps to accommodate your pregnancy?

Yes but that was specific to my manager. A different boss could have handled it differently, but he had children. With the police you do have to advise your senior officer early if you are pregnant, usually well before 12 weeks, because of the risk of conflict in the role. I told my boss I was pregnant but I'd rather wait for the 12 week scan before telling anybody else. He allowed me to say that I had a bad back when I was unwell, which helped.

The change of hours helped because prior to that I'd always worked regular police shifts of 6 days on and 4 days off (2 days, 2 lates and 2 nights). I was still really tired by the time I started maternity leave though. By the eighth month I was shattered and I couldn't cope with the daily grind so I took 2 weeks annual leave and brought the start of my maternity leave forward 2 weeks. And then my baby didn't come for 6 weeks! The little monkey!

I never understood why women wished labour upon themselves until I was 8 months pregnant myself.

Yes and you can't get out of the sofa!

Obviously your baby did eventually arrive. How long were you on maternity leave after the birth?

About 5 months I had with her. She was late coming so I went back when she was 5 months old. I didn't want to go back when she was only 5 months old because I didn't feel ready myself to go back but at the time I felt I had no other choice.

In terms of your reasons for going back to work, they were varied I guess?

Yes for me it was financial. To live where we live location wise is not cheap but also I did want to go back for myself definitely.

Was that because you got a great deal of job satisfaction or was it to do with your own identity?

I think it was probably about my identity. Being in the police is a career for me. I've put so much of my life into it that I didn't want to give it up. Before I knew I was pregnant I'd opted to go back to uniform as part of the promotion process and also because I wanted to work closer to home. My commute used to be a horrible journey! So I had offered myself up to go back to uniform, which at that point no one was doing, and they snapped my hand off!

My request to go back to uniform was made entirely to help with my promotion but it worked in my favour coming back off maternity leave because being "on the beat" meant that I was closer to home.

In my mind I'm imagining you leaving your 5 month old baby in childcare, putting on your uniform and going straight back to front line policing – something you hadn't done for 5 years! How was that?

Probably the most difficult period of my life! Very hard! Obviously it wasn't right for me to go back at 5 months but if you don't have any option and you don't know any different . . . . That's why, with my second child, it was very different. I think you learn your limitations. I know I can't do everything.

How did you negotiate your return to work and decide what hours you wanted to do?

Well I had a friend who'd had a baby a few years before me and she came back on late shifts working Tuesday, Wednesday, Thursday 2.00pm to 12.00 am. Her husband was a salesman, like my husband. So that's where I got the idea.

I took it on my own back to put some structure to my return to work. I contacted work when my daughter was about 2 months old and in that time my boss had changed. I thought

78

I had better go and meet the new Inspector. I'd never worked or dealt with him before so I basically went with what you might call a CV. It gave me the chance to explain to him who I was and what I'd done in the past. I asked to go back to do 3 late shifts on Tuesday, Wednesday, Thursday 2.00 pm till midnight. He took that request away, discussed it with HR and agreed it.

Previously a lot of officers returning from maternity leave would ask for Monday to Friday 9.00am till 5.00pm. I suppose it's quite difficult for married couples in the police but I had the benefit that Ian, my husband, is a Monday to Friday 9.00am to 5.00pm person and not in the police. I said to him all along that if we were trying for a baby then the childcare responsibility had to be split down the middle and he agreed. So he does the child pick up Tuesday, Wednesday and Thursday plus the teatime and bedtime routines and it has worked out well. For me it's no pressure. I can leave to go to work in the afternoon and I know he will pick the girls up and put them to bed. That's a big thing.

So you clock off at midnight. Do you ever have to work overtime?

Sometimes I've been there till 3.00am. It can happen but it doesn't often. If I can get away from work on time then I do because the kids are up at 7.00am and I need some sleep! I'm lucky in that they are good sleepers and they really haven't disturbed me much during the night, which is a blessing with shift work.

Your arrangement means you are at home all day Monday and all day Friday plus mornings Tuesday, Wednesday and Thursday?

Yes although I did recently change my working pattern slightly. I'm now working a day shift every Tuesday. This is so that Ian can go away to customer meetings on Monday, Tuesday or Friday evenings. And it works. However, if my children were light sleepers and up during the night –

forget working till midnight! But even with them being good sleepers, by Friday I'm tired and my eyes are like stalks!

That was my next question. What was it like at home during your re-integration? You've gone through this experience with a really proactive approach. You've requested part-time working, which has been agreed. Your husband is sharing the childcare responsibilities but what is it actually like?

Tiring, but it's a balancing act. My children see more of me this way and I pay less for childcare. I'm still giving time to my work. The downside is that I lose two evenings a week with Ian but we are used to that. We've always had shift work in our lives. That's how our relationship has been from the start and it's not an issue. By Friday I'm cream crackered but . . .

That's take away night!

Yes! Like I said it can't be ideal – it's a compromise

It's making the best of the circumstances?

Yes and I know it won't last for ever because the children are growing all the time but it is hard work at the minute and it will be until they are both school age.

So has your return to work arrangement provided you with the balance you were looking for? I think you are saying "yes it has" but that you were always realistic about what the limitations of that balance would be.

Yes

Would you do anything differently?

Yes, with my second baby I worked as far up to the birth as I could and I kept all my annual leave to bolt onto the end of my maternity leave. I do regret that my second daughter and I have a different bond to me and my first daughter. I think it impacts the first child because you are always worrying about what they are doing and what you should be doing. I've enjoyed my second child more, been more relaxed.

And I guess that your second return to work was better because you knew what to expect and already had a successful part-time working pattern.

Yes, I kept those part-time hours after my second baby. Actually in between babies I got promoted – I've gone into a new role as substantive sergeant. So I got my feet under the table at my new workplace and I knew I wanted to go back there after my second maternity leave. So yes, the second return to work was completely different. I had a female boss when I left who stayed in touch with me by text so it was a hugely different experience.

Is there any advice you would pass on to a new mum going back to work for the first time?

Do what's right for you because we are all different and need different things. You need advice but you are the one who's got to do it and it's got to be right. I think when I went back after my first baby it wasn't a good experience because:

a) she was so young,
b) I wasn't ready and
c) I was also going for promotion and that was a huge amount of additional pressure.

Going back to work is not easy but there is light at the end of the tunnel and it does get easier. They get older and one day my children won't need me. I'll have sent them out into the world and hopefully they will be balanced adults. But I'll still be here with Ian and I keep that in mind. I want to be a person with a career and I want to keep going, hard and tiring though it is. But you do it for yourself and for them.

Key points from Suzy's interview

1) Avoid the deep end on Day 1

Suzy works in the public sector and her interview reflects comments I have heard from other public sector workers such as teachers and nurses. Many mentioned a lack of easing in period for returning mums with little or no re-integration assistance. Obviously this may not be the case in every area of the public sector and sympathetic managers make a big difference, as in Suzy's second return to work, but it would appear that for significant numbers it is pretty much 'GO!' from the first moment back at work. If you suspect your return to work will be like this and would like to experience something different then this book will give you some ideas to discuss with your manager ahead of Day 1 that will help avoid the cold shower sensation that Suzy had.

2) Be proactive if your manager changes while you are away

Suzy's proactive response to a change of manager was very much to her credit. If your manager changes during your maternity leave then do give them a call and go to meet them to introduce yourself. If your new manager has met you, knows a little bit about you and is aware that you are looking forward to working with them it will start to build a relationship and make asking for part-time working much easier later on.

3) Recognise late shift success factors

If you are considering asking for late shifts then make sure you have the same factors in your favour beforehand. Suzy's part-time working arrangement is a success because:

-   Suzy and Ian really do share the childcare workload during the week.
-   Her children are good sleepers. This is fundamental.
-   Suzy has realistic expectations of herself at work and at home.

4) Adopt a long term perspective

Suzy talks about her career in the long term and knows that as her children grow and become more independent things will get easier. Retaining this long term perspective can be a big help when you are tired after a busy day. It does get easier!

<u>Where is Suzy now?</u>

Suzy is still employed as a police sergeant working the same three shift part-time pattern.

Summary of Part 2

While these interviews cannot possibly cover the range of part-time options available to returning mums they have hopefully provided you with valuable insights on both a professional and personal level. You are aware of different classifications to describe flexible working options and you know that these options can be successfully combined into any number of part-time scenarios.

Before these interviews I suggested that you think in terms of the changes you would like to see to your contracted:

Hours

Timing

Location

Role

Hopefully now you are starting to formulate what would be an interesting and workable solution for you as an employee and as a mum too. Don't worry if things are still a little sketchy, by the end of the book you will have gained further clarity about what to ask for and importantly how to ask for it.

This leads us neatly to Part 3 where we will look at negotiation in a lot more detail.

PART 3

How do I negotiate for part-time work?

It's easier than you think!

Does the prospect of conducting a negotiation with your manager about your employment terms put you outside of your comfort zone? If the answer is 'Yes' then, again, you are not alone! In addition to not looking forward to negotiating many mums also feel vulnerable to saying 'Yes' to a working arrangement they really don't want. The key to negotiating is getting into a positive negotiating mindset beforehand. This section focuses on setting you up well from the beginning and thinking positively about the process so that you ask for what you really want and conduct yourself with conviction and professionalism throughout the process.

Let's start with the word 'negotiate'. For some of us just the word alone conjures unhelpful associations. If that is the case with you then change the word 'negotiate' to 'persuade', 'communicate' or 'collaborate'. What you are aiming for here is a mutually beneficial outcome. Only a solution that meets both of your needs is going to work. This means that you need to fully understand and courageously defend your own needs but actively listen to and accommodate your manager's needs too.

This implies using people or interpersonal skills to collaborate in order to get the outcome you are both looking for. Happily this is something in which women tend to excel quite naturally. We are able to pick up subtle cues from body language that tell us when someone is receptive to what we are saying. We are also able to look broadly at options before homing in on a solution. When you start to view the discussion in light of your inbuilt capability it stops being all about you and superficial techniques or clever words and becomes more about jointly finding a way forward using empathy and courage.

We all negotiate, even if we don't recognise that we are doing it. Let's look at how negotiation plays a part in something we all do regularly, shopping. As people we make choices about what we buy and who we 'buy' based on a multitude of elements. How often have you, as a customer, given your business to someone based on the human elements of the deal rather than just the lowest price or longest warranty?

I bought my baby's pram from a small independent store rather than a large national chain because, although they weren't the cheapest, they knew what they were talking about and had time for me. They listened and helped me find a model that really met my personal needs, one that I could easily assemble and disassemble and lift into the boot of my car. They have enjoyed lots of repeat business since then and I'm sure you can think of similar examples of your own.

This human element applies equally in negotiating your part-time working request. The way in which you approach the process and communicate can influence your employer's decision to 'buy' you on part-time terms.

I have listed ten ways in which you can positively affect the outcome of your application. These tips are based in common sense, an understanding of maternity law and personal experience of being both a manager and a working mum. Of course these suggestions are optional and you should feel free to sift this information for what you think will work for you and disregard what you feel will not.

10 tips for negotiating with your manager

The first two steps should ideally be taken before you even leave to have your baby and are:

1. Leave work on a documented high.
2. Pre-agree a communication plan for during maternity leave.

Don't worry if you have not done anything like this and you are already on maternity leave. You can easily start on these now and remember them if there is a next time!

The subsequent six steps are worth considering as you prepare to meet your manager to discuss your return:

3. Get the ball rolling early
4. Have a pre meeting / pre meetings before submitting your application
5. Ask for what you want but be listening for and open minded to alternatives during your meeting
6. Know your negotiable and your non negotiable elements
7. Say 'No' when you need to
8. Check for alignment before you submit your request

The final two steps relate to your negotiations after a decision has been made:

9. If the decision is 'Yes' be prepared to accept a trial period
10. If the decision is 'No' remain on friendly terms and find out what 'No' means.

Let's go back and look at each step in more detail starting with the two steps to take before maternity leave starts:

1) Leave on a documented high!

As you left the office to start your maternity leave the imminent arrival of your baby was probably at the forefront of your mind and having a rest before he or she arrived may have been the only thing on your home based "to do" list. You probably did all you could before you left your workplace to ensure a smooth handover to the person covering your role during your absence. This is a common theme with most mums-to-be not wanting to let their employer down as they depart.

An equally common theme is that mums-to-be don't think too much about setting themselves up for a good return to work after maternity leave and that is what this section is about. Leaving on a documented high is not about being wheeled out into your employer's car park enjoying a heady combination of gas and air! It's about having a positive performance appraisal with your manager before you start your maternity leave. It is likely that you will have done all you can during your pregnancy to be regarded in the best possible light by your customers, your team, your peers and your manager. It is really important that your performance is discussed and documented before you leave so that you and your manager can refer to it when you return to work. Even if the date that you start your maternity leave is well outside the normal appraisal timings it is only fair that you have a proper formal appraisal before you go. This is especially important if your employer would otherwise conduct an appraisal in your absence and use a score or grading from this in the calculation of any performance related bonus.

If you left for maternity leave without having an appraisal or discussing your contribution during your pregnancy then now would be a good time to sit and write some notes to remind yourself of those achievements and contributions. It may help to ring some of your co workers and ask them what they remember of your contribution before you left. You may want to weave some of these examples into your conversation with your manager to refresh his or her memory of what a valuable, conscientious team player you are.

2. Pre-agree a communication plan for during maternity leave.

I'm well aware that as you read this section you are probably already on maternity leave. If you have been in semi regular contact with your manager, that's great! If not, please don't worry about it. It's never too late to pick up the phone or send an email or a text.

Under normal circumstances new mums tend to contact their workplace on three occasions after they have started their maternity leave.

First you send the "He's arrived!" text or email to let everyone know the big event has happened and you are both "doing well!" and you might even send a photo of your new arrival.

Second you send a Thank You card for any gifts or flowers that arrive from colleagues.

Finally there is the almost obligatory visit to work a little later to introduce your new baby.

I did these three things, but that was about it. I did not have any conversation with my manager about communication before I left on maternity leave. I then had no contact with him at all for 8 months. As a result I did feel very much on the back foot when I then came to ask for part-time working. In hindsight I would definitely have spent some time discussing how much or how little contact I would have liked to have. I would certainly have phoned or emailed every couple of months to gently remind my manager of my existence and my interest in what was going on within the team and the wider company.

Although there is no legal requirement to stay in touch and every excuse under the circumstances to waddle out and not give work a second thought for up to 12 months do bear in mind that part-time working requests can be influenced by your manager's perception of your contribution and commitment. The old adage "out of sight out, out of mind" really does apply here. The perception back in the office of even a star employee will fade over time so be proactive, don't lose touch completely.

Having laboured the point about staying in touch to some degree what are your options for staying in touch? The table below provides some options for consideration.

Staying in touch suggestions
a) If you are keeping a laptop and mobile phone you might consider managing the expectations of your boss and colleagues by letting them know that you intend to check emails and phone messages only semi regularly and prefer to be regarded as an observer of what is going on rather than a participant. Many sleep deprived mums find that these two items gather dust somewhere in their house during maternity leave. Don't worry if that happens to you too.
b) Ask to maintain access to your company intranet, if there is one, so you can dust your laptop off and log on occasionally to read the latest company internal news. This helps keep you connected with the business as a whole.
c) Request your HR team let you know about any vacancies that would be of interest to you during your maternity leave. You will have to define what would be of interest. You are entitled to ask for this and entitled to apply for vacancies whilst on maternity leave. It might be that a part-time vacancy arises that would suit you very well. Obviously this type of activity can be governed by company protocol (and certainly by professional etiquette) requiring you to inform your line manager first. In some companies it is possible to view vacancies speculatively via an intranet and only if you decide to apply for a new role does your line manager need to be advised.

d) Request notification from your HR team or your line manager about all relevant structural / organisational changes that occur within the company during your maternity leave. Again you are entitled to ask for this.

e) Talk with your manager about finding a way for you to be kept up to date, on a semi regular basis, with regard to key projects, company performance or anything else important to you while you are on maternity leave. This might be achieved by organising a phone call every few months for a chat or receiving an email that you can read when you have time. A quick chat should identify what will work for both of you as a manageable means of communication.

f) Ask to be invited, while on maternity leave, to the company conference or to team training courses (Keep In Touch days could be used here). Also consider asking to be invited to any social out of work events such as welcoming new team members down the pub, saying goodbye to those leaving or retiring plus of course the annual Christmas Party. Taking part in the fun stuff can help you to re-integrate even more quickly when you go back.

Quite honestly you will not really know the level of contact you want to have with your workplace until your baby arrives and you can explain that without causing any offence. You do not need to feel guilty if you decide to trim the level of communication at a later date. People will understand.

The goal here with regard to contact and communication is to ensure that you are viewed as a remote but never-the-less interested party in your company's progress. Out of sight but not out of mind. On maternity leave not on holiday. If the suggestions above just don't work for you, that's fine. I'm sure you can think of lots of ways to ensure that people are thinking about you. Whatever you decide to do with regard to contact with your workplace make your decisions based on an appreciation of the implications of doing too little.

You can decide how you want to be perceived during your maternity leave and you can exert that influence through contact and communication.

If you are reading this as you approach the end of your maternity leave and you have made no contact at all with your line manager during your leave then don't worry – it really is never too late to start. Consider getting in touch in some way today. Send a short sociable email or make a phone call, even if it's just for a quick chat. You don't need to discuss your return to work at all if you feel under prepared to do so. Just be interested in what is going on in his or her world and listen to your manager's latest news. Alternatively you could use this as an opportunity to say that you are considering asking for flexible working and, although your ideas are in their early stages, you would appreciate a copy of your job description to help that process.

Steps 3 through to 10 are negotiation tips for mums already on maternity leave.

3) Get the ball rolling early

Most employers will assume that a mum will take the full 52 weeks for maternity leave. If you want to return to work before the end of 52 weeks your employer is entitled to 8 weeks notice before your desired date of return. It would be wise to add a few more weeks notice to that if you intend to request a part-time working pattern. I would suggest giving 12 weeks notice as a minimum.

This point has already been mentioned but it is worth re stating. Your employer will need time to meet with you to discuss part-time options, more time to go away and consider your verbal request and then even more time to meet internally and process your formal written application. Your application will be very high on your priority list. It will be vital to you that it goes well. For your manager it may still be important but it will be another item on their long "To Do" list. Starting the process well before your desired return date and allowing plenty of time for consideration, inevitable bureaucracy and possible additional meetings will go in your favour.

4) The importance of a meeting (or several meetings) before submitting your request.

Let's return to our characters Anna and Paul and imagine the scenario below:

Anna has been on maternity leave for 9 months and intends to return to work after 12 months. Prior to having her baby Anna was contracted to work 5 days a week Monday to Friday 9.00am till 5.00pm. She would like to return to work on a 4 day basis working Tuesday to Friday 9.00am to 5.00pm. She contacts her manager, Paul, and arranges a meeting. At the meeting Anna has opportunity to catch up with the latest happenings in the office such as the staff changes and learn about the new IT project. She has the chance to broach the topic of part-time working, make her suggestion and gauge Paul's reaction. The meeting gives Paul the chance to start thinking about how a 4 day week might work before a written application is received. Importantly this meeting also gives each party the chance to reacquaint themselves with important factors such as:

For Anna – the reasons why she wants to go back to work and be part of Paul's team.

For Paul – the reasons why he wants Anna back in his team and the value that Anna could bring on a reduced hours basis.

During the meeting Paul advises Anna that her application would be better if it was a request to work Monday to Thursday. This better meets the needs of the office which encounters a heavy workload on a Monday but generally has a quieter day on a Friday. From Anna's perspective she is happy because she still has 3 consecutive days with her baby. Anna recognizes that her part-time working arrangement needs to work for her employer too.

A few weeks later, after a number of telephone calls with Paul, Anna sends Paul her refined official flexible working request for a part-time role. During the previous telephone conversations Paul suggested that Anna pass a number of her responsibilities on to Tina, who has been covering these areas well and growing as a result. Anna had asked if she could pick up a number of her ex colleague's responsibilities to provide her with manageable new stretch. Paul verbally agreed and Anna's application contains these jointly formulated suggestions. Anna's original application idea has been significantly amended following the conversations she has had with Paul but she has increased peace of mind in making the application because it has been made in consultation with her manager, who ultimately needs to approve it. It is therefore less likely to be rejected.

How different would the outcome have been if Anna had simply sent a letter to Paul without any prior contact? Paul would have received the request with no prior warning or warm up. It would be asking for a 4 day working week that excluded the busiest day. Paul's response might be influenced by the abrupt nature of the application and would certainly be affected by the lack of consideration for the needs of the business.

The above example highlights that there is simply no substitute for a face-to-face meeting with your manager before submitting a request for a part-time working pattern. There is a very good reason why the legal clock starts ticking only once the request is made in writing. Both parties have the opportunity to discuss options openly before an application is made. This way the employer has more time to consider the request and possibly make alternative suggestions that are more workable within the business. The end result will be a refined application that recognizes the needs of each party and that is more likely to be agreed.

One other point worth mentioning here, when you have your meeting with your manager, go alone!

I had one rather comical pre meeting with my manager before I submitted my own part-time working request. My workplace was quite a drive from my home so my manager suggested we meet half way in a suitable location, a lovely country hotel with corporate meeting facilities. At that time my daughter was not yet at nursery and my parents lived hundreds of miles away. A family friend I trusted as a babysitter was away on a last minute holiday so I felt I had little choice other than to take my baby with me. I rang my boss to explain my daughter would be coming along too.

"Don't worry!" he reassured me. "You won't be the first mum to bring their baby to this sort of meeting!"

In hindsight it would have been better if I had re scheduled the meeting until the family friend was available to help. My baby's presence in the meeting was distracting for me and made it difficult to concentrate on presenting myself as the valuable returning professional. My boss had brought along a thick pack of presentation notes and business results to take me through. Showing engagement and understanding while bouncing my baby on my knee and waggling her teddy to keep her entertained wasn't the best way to convince my boss he needed me back in his team. Thankfully she didn't need a nappy change!

The recommendation is obvious. If you are able to leave your baby with someone you trust for the few hours it may take to meet with your manager, then do so. Your meeting will be far more productive, trust me!

5) Ask for what you want but listen for and stay open minded to alternative suggestions.

It is for you to decide the number of days that you would prefer to work on a part-time basis and finances will probably play a role in that decision. The greater the difference between what you want to ask for and your previous working arrangement, the harder it may feel to ask for it. Despite this, it is really important that in your initial conversation with your manager you do ask for what you want, even if that means practicing in front of the bathroom mirror beforehand!

"I was thinking of applying for flexible working to work ABC days from X am to Z pm. I would like to explore how that might work for both of us and the team."

If he or she says 'No' at this initial verbal stage, you have lost nothing! You can continue conversation until you find common ground. If you don't ask you will always wonder, "What if . . ."

As with Anna's scenario it may become clear through conversation that you need to revise part of your request because it is not workable for your employer. It may be that your manager has a different role in mind for you when you go back and it may be one that would be more manageable on part-time hours. Being open minded at this stage may help you to arrive at a more acceptable proposal for everyone.

If during the course of conversation your manager makes a suggestion or counter proposal then the likelihood is that they are alluding to another option or solution that they would accept as a part-time working arrangement. Listen out for it and explore it.

Don't be afraid to ask questions such as:

- Which days, in your view, are the busiest days of the week at work?
- What elements of my role have successfully been re assigned during my maternity leave?
- What is your opinion of home working?
- What are the biggest challenges / opportunities facing the team at the moment?
- I'm open to doing a different role in your team, do you have any vacancies?

The answers to these questions will help to shape and inform your application. Without answers to questions such as these your application is based purely around what works for you and your perception of what your manager needs, which may be correct or incorrect.

6) Know your negotiable and your non negotiable elements

Before you meet with your manager think carefully about the different aspects of your desired working pattern. There may be some that are fundamental to you and others that are nice to have. Having this level of clarity is valuable for both you and your manager. Here are some examples.

Some mums are quite happy to work whatever 3 days their manager requires, just as long as it is only 3 days and not 4 days.

Some mums are happy to accommodate an early start, even at short notice, but not happy to finish late.

Some mums will happily do overtime but really do not want to do business travel.

While being open minded and flexible are important it is equally useful to know what would cause you problems. Wherever these elements exist try to have a counter point that helps you to demonstrate to your manager that you want to meet in the middle. Help him or her to see that, while you have new constraints, you are still able to be flexible in other useful ways.

7) Say 'No' when you need to

Be prepared to say 'No' to a proposal or part of a proposal that you know will not give you the balance you are looking for. It requires courage to do this but consider the consequences of agreeing to a proposal that will make you tired, stressed and miserable. Don't settle for what you know will tip your life out of balance. What constitutes a situation of balance is different for each of us. As long as you are comfortable with your definition and defend it that is all that matters.

> "A 'No' uttered from deepest conviction is better and greater than a 'Yes' merely uttered to please, or what is worse, to avoid trouble."
>
> - Mahatma Gandhi

If your employer requests that you return to work under terms that you really don't want, then respectfully say 'No' and explain why that suggestion is not something you can agree to. Without wanting to patronize the following phrase might help if you feel under pressure to capitulate.

"I'm committed to finding a solution that works for both of us but part of this proposal concerns me because I think it will make it difficult for me to perform well and achieve the balance I'm looking for. Can I explain the aspects that are concerning me and why and can we jointly look for some solutions or alternatives?"

This keeps the channels open and enables you to share your concerns constructively. It could mean that you need to schedule another meeting at a later date to discuss your return further and allow you and your manager time to think about what other options might be or how your concerns can be addressed.

8) Check for alignment before you submit your request

Before you put your request in writing you need to have confidence that it will be agreed. Which managerial response fills you with most certainty of success?

Phrase A
"Put your request in writing and I'll talk about it back at the office, have a think and let you know."

Phrase B
"I'm glad we've had this chat. I think your proposal will work for both of us. Put it in writing and we'll process it"

If your manager ends your negotiation discussions with a phrase that most closely mirrors Phrase A then I would suggest that you don't have his or her full support. It would be wise to either engage in further dialogue or allow him or her time to discuss the proposal back at the office and come back to you with feedback before you submit anything.

There is no reason why you cannot reach a point of verbal agreement over your revised terms such that the application and processing are mere formalities. Ensure that you and your manager are aligned before you submit your request.

In addition to reaching agreement on your new working pattern it is also important that you reach agreement with your manager about how your new working pattern can be accommodated within the team. If you remember back to the legal section in Part 1 you learned that it is your responsibility to make suggestions about how any redistribution of responsibilities is accommodated. The phrase from the legislation was:

> Indicate how you think this will impact on the business and make recommendations as to how your employer can reduce or remove any impact.

This part of the legislation is, in my opinion, poorly conceived. Your manager will be well aware that you have been out of the workplace for a significant period. During that time much might have changed. Your recommendations are likely to be based upon how the workplace operated before you left, possibly making them outdated. There is a simple way to avoid making that mistake – simply ask your manager or your team if anything significant has changed during your maternity leave that would make your recommendations outdated. If things have changed then discuss these factors with your manager.

There will be one factor in particular that you will have a thorough understanding of and you will be able to make very relevant recommendations about how it is accommodated. I am referring to your previous levels of overtime, especially if you did habitual overtime before your baby arrived.

To put this into a more real context let's look at how Anna assessed her previous working pattern and compared it to the new one she was negotiating for.

Previously she worked a full-time 40 hour week. She wanted Paul to agree to a part-time 32 hour week. The difference of 8 hours or 20% seems manageable with a small re adjustment of responsibilities until you get under the skin of her previous working reality.

Anna knows she used to work 1 hour of overtime everyday, finishing at 6.00pm most nights. This was fine before she had Daniel but now she will need to leave promptly to collect him. Anna is happy to do overtime occasionally but habitual overtime is not something she now wants to do.

Analysed in this way you can see that she used to work 45 hours a week and is proposing to reduce this to 32 hours. In reality her hours are dropping 29%.

I don't intend to argue the rights and wrongs of this situation. The point I am making is that it is important not to gloss over it during your negotiations. When we care about our careers we work the hours that are required to feel as though we are doing a good job. If that previously meant that you did lots of extra hours then some significant amounts of work may need to be re assigned to make your proposed drop in hours workable, unless you still plan to do the same amount of overtime, which some women do.

If you are returning to the same role on part-time hours then it is really important that you discuss up front:

- The real drop in hours
- Which tasks you would no longer have the time to do and

- How these tasks can be re-allocated within your team / re designed to save you time / absorbed by another team / outsourced / dropped altogether etc.

It is not unreasonable for you to table this frankly with your manager and suggest that you collaborate on an effective responsibility re-distribution solution. Monitoring how well this is going once you are back will be an important part of your successful re-integration so being explicit about this will be well worth it later on.

Once you have alignment in these two areas then you are able to write and submit your request.

The two final tips relate to your negotiations after a decision has been reached.

9) If the decision is 'Yes' be prepared to accept a trial period

If your application is processed and the decision comes back as:

"Yes, but we'd like to trial this new way of working first."

Say "Ok, thank you!" Basically your employer has agreed your application and your previous terms and conditions have been superseded. Any subsequent review can only look at how to improve the new way of working. That means your employer cannot revert back to your old terms if they decide during or after the trial period that the new working pattern, or part of it, is proving unsuccessful. You will both need to get around the table and collaborate on a more workable part-time solution.

Worth noting is that although the length of a trial period is not set out in law a reasonable trial period is considered by legal experts to be 3 months. It is also reasonable to expect to meet with your line manager every month during the trial to review progress otherwise, through what is called 'custom and practice' the new way of working could reasonably be considered to have been a success for both of you.

10) If the decision is 'No' then remain on friendly terms and find out what 'No' means.

Getting a 'No' can be a big disappointment and quite a shock but this is not the end of the story so don't see it as such. We have all met sales representatives who see a 'No' as the start point in the sales process. In this situation it is really important that you do not take a 'No' personally. It is only a 'No' to the request you submitted. It is not a reflection on you as a person. There may be workplace reasons behind it that no one could have foreseen that have influenced the decision at last minute. I encourage you to adopt a resilient attitude and stay optimistic. Part 5 offers detailed guidance should you find yourself in this situation and real life experiences for you to draw upon. Don't worry, there are options.

If asking for part-time working still feels like a big deal then do ask for support from friends and family while you are going through this process. It may be your partner, a close family member or a trusted work colleague. Find someone who you can share the journey with, who can give you objective feedback about the working pattern you are considering and above all, make sure you choose someone who is a positive thinker.

Well-balanced recipe 1:
A Part-time Working Request

By now you have a better understanding of:

- How and why you may feel as you do about going back to work
- What might be going through your manager's mind during the process
- What other mums have done in designing their part-time working pattern
- Many of the options available when applying for part-time working
- The legal requirements in the application procedure
- How you can positively influence the outcome during the negotiation

This being the case, you are now able to go into the kitchen and start baking recipe 1. You are able to select part-time working pattern ingredients with a heightened understanding of how they work in practice, giving due consideration to what you want, why you want it and why your manager will be happy to agree to it. You will still need to plan a meeting with your manager to discuss these ingredient ideas but you can start to formulate a discussion.

You are able to present your suggestions to your manager in a collaborative manner and recognise that the final solution needs to accommodate both your needs and his or her needs. You are able to spot signals that tell you whether your discussion is leading to agreement on a new working pattern and you know it is ok to ask for another meeting in a week or so if you both need time to think, to consult or to investigate alternative options.

Once the ingredients for your changed working pattern are verbally agreed you are able to bake it to perfection in the form of an appropriately structured and compelling letter or email positively presenting your request. Just to recap the vital elements that need to go into this document are statements that make clear that you are:

- making a flexible working request in order to care for your baby.
- asking for a revised working pattern i.e. a change to your hours, location, timing or role.
- requesting a specific start date giving appropriate notice.
- acknowledging how this change may affect your employer and your team.
- making suggestions to minimise the impact.
- noting if and when any previous flexible working requests have been made.

You are ready. You are capable. You will do an excellent job.

Summary of Part 3

Part 3 recognised that negotiation does not come easily to all of us. If you recognise yourself as being a nervous negotiator then Part 3 has shown how changing your mindset on this topic, before you even get started, is very helpful.

Part of this mindset change involves recognising that negotiation forms part of your everyday life and how, as a woman, you are very capable at picking up the subtle cues of body language that tell you when a conversation is on track.

In reality you will be collaborating with your manager to find a win-win working pattern. This removes a lot of unnecessary pressure and infers that you are equal partners in your discussions.

The ten tips for negotiating provide you with suggestions that will enable you to approach conversations with your manager in a professional and thorough manner. The ten tips are listed again below:

The first two steps should ideally be taken before you even leave to have your baby and are:

1. Leave work on a documented high.
2. Agree a communication plan for during maternity leave.

The subsequent six steps are worth considering as you prepare to meet your manager to discuss your return:

3. Get the ball rolling early.
4. Have a pre meeting or pre meetings before submitting your application.
5. Ask for what you want but listen for and stay open minded to alternatives during your meeting.

6. Know your negotiable and your non negotiable elements.
7. Say 'No' when you need to.
8. Check for alignment before you submit your request.

The final two steps relate to your negotiations after your employer's decision has been made:

9. If the decision is 'Yes' be prepared to accept a trial period.
10. If the decision is 'No' then remain on friendly terms and find out what 'No' means.

It is highly likely that your application will be agreed at this point. Once you have reached this stage the next logical step is to start building your personal support plan. Onward to Part 4!

PART 4

Support sounds great!
What support?

Ask and you will receive!

Asking for support at work and at home isn't rocket science but so many of us don't do it because we don't know what help to ask for. Thankfully with a bit of guidance that can easily be changed. We are back in the kitchen at this point.

Energizing recipe 2:
A Re-integration Support Proposal

Whenever I think about this recipe I always imagine a healthy fruit smoothie. For this recipe you need to choose the ingredients that appeal to you personally from a wide selection of options. You will then put your proposal to your manager and collaborate to determine which 'fruit' from your selection are available at your workplace. Once agreed you can then blend these options and turn your proposal into your own personal energizing smoothie or re-integration support plan.

The mere act of creating a re-integration support plan with your manager has numerous benefits enabling you to:

- play a proactive part in your return to work
- reconnect with your professional identity
- allow you to collaborate positively with your line manager on a topic of mutual benefit and re establish your working relationship
- help you to re-integrate quickly and achieve high performance earlier.
- reduce any stress you may be feeling before and during your return to work
- increase your level of engagement to your company

Having a support plan in place can help turn dread into happy anticipation because you will know that going back to work will not be like taking a cold shower. Rather it will be like gradually easing yourself into a simple yoga position that you used to be able to do well. It may take practice to feel comfortable but you know what you are aiming for and you know it is achievable.

Every woman I have worked with has taken the 10 suggestions below and built on them to reflect their own situation. As a result every re-integration support proposal has been different so please take their lead and use these suggestions to spark your own ideas. Be creative and remember – if you don't ask, you don't get!

1) Keep In Touch days (KIT days)

These are the most obvious option to provide you with support as you return to work. They can be used before the return to work without bringing maternity leave to an end. You can use all or some of the 10 days available, with prior agreement from your employer, and they can be used in many different ways including.

- ongoing training during maternity leave
- helping with a gradual re introduction back to the workplace as you resume responsibilities over time
- meeting new colleagues / team members
- attending company conferences / trade shows
- understanding how your role may have changed during your maternity leave so you can formulate a better part-time working proposal.

KIT days are a great way to re-integrate but do make sure that you clarify with your company whether or not you will be paid for them as payment is entirely discretionary. Many companies offer a full days pay for every KIT day, whether you are working a full day or only a few hours. It would be worth establishing what your company's policy is beforehand.

2) Reduced hours in first week

Most employers appreciate that your first week back is likely to be a challenge for you and your baby. If you ask for reduced hours in the first week it is likely that your employer will be happy to allow you to start a little later and finish a little earlier. Most of the women I have worked with have made this request successfully and gained the following benefits:

- This allows you time to acclimatise yourself to getting you and your baby ready and out of the door as part of your new morning routine without joining the peak of rush hour.
- Equally it allows you to leave your workplace early to collect your baby and settle them gradually into their new afternoon/ evening routine.
- Finally it gives you time to get used to the demands of being a working mum.

3) Flexible hours

If your employer is not willing to allow you to work reduced hours in your first week then they may consider allowing you to flex the hours slightly for example you might:

- start an hour earlier and finish an hour earlier (spend more time with your baby in the afternoon / evening)
- start an hour later and finish an hour later (slower start to the day / avoid the morning rush hour)

You may need to check that this option is workable for your childcare provider before requesting it of your manager.

4) Well timed and extended hand back of responsibilities

If your manager has employed someone to cover your maternity leave it is worth asking whether that person would be able to stay on to conduct a professional and thorough hand back. You might request that your maternity cover continues for a number of weeks after your return thereby enabling you to benefit from a thorough and appropriately paced hand back of responsibilities. This is especially useful if there have been significant changes to your role or systems that you need to use. If your role involves detailed financial reporting at the end of each month you might want to co-ordinate the timing of your return so that your maternity cover is there to take you through any changes that have occurred during your absence.

5) New Starter Induction Request

Would you like to be treated as a new starter and receive a new starter style induction? If the answer is 'Yes', then here is the place to ask for it. Be aware of the short comings of this as an option as well as the benefits. We covered this in Part 1 on page 27.

6) Training Requests / Refresher Courses

Many women feel they need a recap on something when they return to work after maternity leave. The type of training you may want to request will obviously depend upon your profession and whether you are returning to the same or a different role. Examples I have come across are listed below to prompt your own thoughts.

Lawyers requesting updates on changes to legislation or new precedents set in case law.

Doctors seeking updates on drugs, protocols, patient procedures and targets.

Office workers receiving training on updated systems or new procedures.

By far the most unusual refresher training request I have encountered was for battlefield telecommunications and weapons from a mum employed as a Major in the Army!

7) Maternity coaching

Coaching is a process whereby, through 1 to 1 conversation, a person is able to recognise personal barriers, find clarity, discern options, determine an alternative way forward and become personally motivated to make changes in order to improve some area of their life.

More and more companies recognise that the return to work after maternity leave is a huge life change. Maternity coaching is being offered to support female employees as they transition back to their job. It may be that the coaching is provided by an in-house coach or an external coach. Regardless of the source it is worth asking for it if you think it will be of benefit. Remember, if you were leaving a big company due to redundancy then outplacement support would be provided or even expected and that costs money. Investing in appropriate support for you as you return to work will increase your loyalty to the company and improve your ability to manage the change process. Surely that makes the cost a worthwhile investment. The number of coaching sessions you have and the frequency of them is not something set in stone. Some people opt to have one coaching session a month for 6 months, while others prefer a short sharp burst of support over the first 3 months. Individual coaching sessions usually take 1 hour or slightly longer, certainly no longer than 2 hours.

A key success factor in coaching is having good rapport with your coach so make sure that you feel the coach assigned is:

- Qualified to support you as you take responsibility for managing significant change.
- Able to credibly participate in discussions that might well range outside of work into your home life and the world of babies.
- The right person to help you to stay positive, learn and achieve great results.

8) Request a Return-to-Work Buddy

Normally a return-to-work buddy is another working mum in your company who has been through the return experience. The benefit of assigning you a buddy is that instead of bottling up any concerns you may have you can share them with someone who is well placed to help you to find solutions or just re assure you that what you are feeling is normal and will ease over time.

This differs from participating in a women's network because the primary goal is not to help you to make contacts and achieve promotion. The objective is to provide you with a positive working mum role model you can confide in and trust.

It is vital that this person is a positive influence and knows that their role is to help you to find your feet and encourage you to keep going. It is also vital that you have confidence that what you discuss will remain between you.

9) Breastfeeding: privacy for expressing and facilities for cold storage

If you intend to continue breastfeeding your baby after you return to work and you need to express milk during the day to maintain flow then let your employer know before you go back to work. Your employer will need to provide you with appropriate facilities (a private room where you can express and access to a fridge for storage). Your employer will need to ensure that these facilities are in place for your first day back, so it is only fair to advise them in good time in case provision needs to be arranged.

Reasonable time away from your work to express is also covered by legislation however you will need to discuss this with your employer to agree between you what constitutes 'reasonable' and when this will occur.

If you are lucky enough to have a nursery at your place of work or childcare nearby then you may be able to agree with your employer that you can leave work to breastfeed your baby and then return to work afterwards.

Tips to consider:

- If your workplace operates using an electronic diary system then block time in your day as 'busy' when you need to be expressing or feeding so that it cannot be filled with meetings.

- Tell key colleagues what you doing so that you don't get delayed by corridor meetings en route to your baby or your pump!

- If you are planning to use breast milk storage bags then consider putting them into a second container, such as a sandwich box, for extra security in the fridge.

10) Request a meeting your line manager on your first day / first week.

This one seems obvious but it is surprising how many returning women don't prioritise it. A positive and productive re-integration meeting with your manager either on your first day but certainly during your first week will help to set the tone for your return. Topics for discussion that are useful for you to put on the agenda include:

- You and your baby and how you are both adjusting to the new routine (including whether your baby is sleeping through the night yet or not).
- An update for your manager on how your re-integration support plan is helping you.
- What you can see has changed while you've been away.
- A brief business performance update from your manager.
- A discussion on how your manager wants you to handle child sickness when it occurs e.g. work from home or take a day of holiday.
- Clarity about any agreed changes to your role and responsibilities.
- Pointers from your manager about what he or she needs you to focus on in the next few weeks.
- Your manager's priorities for the year and how you and your role fit into delivering his or her priorities.

- Your objectives for the year or what remains of the year (do you adopt the objectives of the person who provided maternity cover or create your own).

Presenting your manager with a return to work support proposal before you go back will help to position you in a very good light. It demonstrates you still have your 'edge', remain committed to your company and your manager and want to achieve high performance as early as possible.

Calming recipe 3:
A Home Support Plan

This recipe is, to my mind, akin to homemade soup on a cold day or a special herbal tea infusion. You can sense yourself slowing down and embracing calm as you taste a few spoonfuls or as you put your hands around your hot mug and breathe the scented vapour.

In the same way that you have proactively created a work place support proposal to discuss with your manager this section encourages you to think about a similar plan, tailored to your home, that you can create yourself and discuss with family and friends.

The goal is to help you to break down the change that is coming into smaller parts and plan for it. This will enable you to turn nagging worry about a significant life change into a considered plan. Feeling prepared and organised is a great antidote to dreading the unknown and, as mentioned before, it releases you to enjoy every single day of your maternity leave.

There are a number of ways in which you can support yourself by thinking ahead and imagining how your working day / week might unfold. All the returning mums who have used this home support framework have found it helpful to spark their own ideas and they then created a plan that met their individual needs and circumstances. Please feel free to follow their lead.

We will look at this in terms of how you can help yourself during:

- the last few weeks before you go back to work
- the day before you go back to work
- the night before
- the months to come after your return to work

We will also look at how you can enlist the help of:

- friends and family
- your husband / partner and pets!

You might want your pen handy for this section too for highlighting suggestions that appeal or scribbling your own ideas as they come to you.

Helping yourself in the last few weeks of maternity leave

1) Childcare induction for baby, building your separation tolerance.

Your baby's childcare induction could start a few days ahead of your return to work or a few weeks before. Remember that this induction is for you too! This may be the first time that you have been apart from your baby for a lengthy period. If you are leaving your baby with a family member then that may be a little easier but I would still recommend an easing in plan. Essentially it is really important that you do whatever works for you and your baby to make your first proper day back at work as easy as possible for both of you.

The nursery who looked after my daughter advised me that a three day gradual induction would be sufficient for my daughter. Her induction went like this:

Day 1: My daughter spent 20 minutes with the nursery team without me, but I was close by in another room.

Day 2: My daughter spent 1 hour with the nursery team without me and I was doing the weekly shop.

Day 3: My daughter spent half a day with the nursery team without me while I was wondering what to do with myself and missing her.

This approach worked well enough for my baby and the nursery team but it did not work for me. In hindsight it would have been better for me if I had requested an induction over a longer period that built up to my leaving her there for a whole working day. An ex colleague of mine started the nursery induction process four weeks before her own return to work so that, by the time she started work, going to nursery was something that she and her baby were already well used to. This also meant that she had opportunity to start to get to grips with the morning routine before doing it for real. I would probably have benefited from doing something similar. We are all different though, so do what works for both you and your baby. If finances don't allow you to use chargeable childcare in the run up to your return perhaps you can find a friend or family member who can help you to build up your separation tolerance.

2) Baby supplies agreed and organised

Have a chat with your childcare provider so you know what baby supplies to bring on your child's first day. Items might include:

- nappies
- teething gel
- nappy rash cream
- wipes
- change of baby clothes x 2
- familiar cuddly toy
- familiar cuddly blanket
- bottle and teats

3) Reassurance telephone calls

Most childcare providers are well used to mothers calling regularly to check on their babies in the first few weeks of going back to work. Some may ask that you avoid ringing at busy drop off or collection times but will otherwise be very happy for you to ring for an update.

4) Feedback from your childcare provider at the end of the day

Establish what sort of update and feedback you will get from your childcare provider to keep you up to date with what has been going on during your baby's day. This helps enormously when you collect them after work. Most nurseries will provide you with a written daily summary telling you

- what your baby ate and drank
- when they slept and for how long
- nappy events
- games and toys that your baby played with
- any new skills observed such as crawling, rolling over

Whoever is providing childcare you may want to establish up front what you would like to know about at the end of each day although obviously if a member of your family is your childcare provider then it may not be such a formal arrangement or involve a written summary.

5) Understand your childcare provider's flexibility regarding overtime

Although working overtime may not be high on your wish list there may come a time when you will need to either drop baby off early or collect later than usual. Understanding in advance the extent of your childcare flexibility is hugely valuable and sharing that information with your manager and co workers is even more valuable.

6) Think through the activities and timings of your new morning routine.

When do you need to set your morning alarm to get yourself and your baby up and ready and out of the house? Will you shower in the morning or the night before? Will you put your work outfit on immediately after your shower or return to your dressing gown and only get dressed for work the moment before you leave? Just bear in mind that no matter how well you think you have planned this bit – it will always be different on the day and probably everyday for a while. Running late is all part of learning the ropes. Don't panic! Just keep going purposefully in the right direction. You will no doubt forget something and you will probably find you have a splodge of baby food on your jacket or talc on your trousers as you get into work. This is all normal and it does get better over time.

One important aspect of your Day 1 morning routine is your outfit. My first choice Day 1 outfit didn't fit me any more but thankfully I had that rather depressing realisation well before the first morning and avoided a headless chicken moment! Trying your work clothes on before Day 1 is even more important if you wear a uniform and would need to contact work to organise comfortable clothing to be available for your return.

7) Buy the weekly shop before you go back to work and have a meal plan for the week ahead.

We have all heard about cooking ahead and freezing batches of the same dish to make life easy. Despite being a cliché it can be a lifesaver when you are tired and hungry. Having an idea of what you are going to eat during your first week in the form of a meal plan is also useful but there are other options too such as:

- take away – there is a time and a place and it is here and now!
- microwave dinners – ok so it's not politically correct to mention, but we all do it from time to time.

- your other half doing the cooking.
- going to family or friends nearby for your evening meal.
- friends or family coming over to your house to do the cooking for you.

Some of these options may require some forward planning but if they are pre arranged they can help to take the pressure off you when you feel shattered. Knowing that you don't have to cook at the end of the day can help you get to the finish line at work in far better shape.

8) Set up an on-line grocery shopping account

Once you have set this up with your chosen retailer it means that you don't need to set foot in a supermarket ever again if you don't want to. We've all done the supermarket trip with the baby who grizzles the whole way round the store then needs a nappy change just as you empty your trolley contents onto the checkout conveyor belt. Even if you just shop on line once and save your items as favourites it can help in the future if, for example, your child becomes sick and you are housebound nursing them.

9) Stock up on treats for you

We all need a little boost occasionally and your first week back at work is definitely the time to give yourself some well earned rewards. Going back to work is a major change to your routine and mummy treats are a must. Make sure you stock up on whatever you consider a reward because you will deserve it!

10) Get closure on your maternity leave

I recommend that you give this suggestion serious consideration. Maternity leave is such a precious time and as it draws to a close it is really worth planning a little family something or other to recognise that it is ending and a new phase is starting. It could be a picnic in the park, a weekend away to see friends or family, an outing to a local beauty spot. Some families go to a professional photographer and capture the moment that way. Taking a few photos and celebrating how far you've come are really useful ways to get closure. Having a baby and raising a child is a big deal – do some self congratulating, some looking back with pride on the months that have been your maternity leave. Think about what you've learned, the challenges you have overcome, how your life has changed, how hard you've worked. Know that you've done a great job! This helps you draw a line under your maternity leave and create an emotional spring board to move forward.

Helping yourself the day before you go back to work

This is when you can do little things to set yourself up well for the working days to come. It includes doing jobs well ahead of time and just being more organised than usual.

1) Laying out your pre chosen work outfit the night before

Just laying your clothes out somewhere ready for the next morning can help you to feel calmer and win you time.

2) Selecting your baby's daycare clothes the night before (plus two spare sets.)

It sounds obvious but anything that saves you time on that first day is worth doing. One further point to make here is that as long as your baby is clothed, comfortable and warm enough it really doesn't matter how trendy or cute they look when they go to childcare. I stopped counting the number of times I dropped my baby off in mismatched clothes because the top part or bottom part of her perfectly co-ordinated outfit had gotten dirty just before we left the house. Whatever you dress your baby in, they won't stay clean for long and when you collect your baby you will probably be handed a little nappy bag with some dirty clothes inside that will create a wonderful aroma in your car on the way home. Childcare does not need to be a baby show!

3) Ensuring you have petrol in the car for the week ahead

Ok so not everyone uses a car to get to work but however you commute think about how you might make it a smoother experience. One client told me that she intended to walk her child to nursery and then walk from the nursery to work everyday. She bought her baby a second hand off-road style pram and had it serviced. She bought herself some new trainers and a pink high visibility vest and looked up the local bus times for whenever it was raining. However you intend to get yourself and your baby to your respective destinations in the morning there may be things that you can do ahead of time to feel prepared.

4) Putting some tissues, mascara and soothing eye gel in your handbag

It's ok to cry. It's even better to cry if you are able to cool your hot eyes, touch up your mascara, smile in the mirror and keep going.

5) Have access to some pre chosen uplifting music

If you plan to listen to music during your journey to work don't rely on the radio to be uplifting. Music has the ability to really settle you so however you commute take the opportunity to choose something that you know will put you in a good state of mind as you travel. This will need doing before hand but knowing that it's there waiting for you will be calming.

Helping yourself the night before you go back to work

1) Relax and unwind

Obviously you need to get your rest before you go back to work and it is only natural that you might feel a little nervous. Putting steps in place to help you to relax and feel prepared can help a great deal. That might include:

- a delicious evening meal, one of your favourite dishes

- a gentle film that you know will help you to switch off and unwind
- a friendly chat on the phone with family or friends who are positive people
- a relaxing bubbly bath with candles
- an absorbing uplifting book
- preparing your bag and baby's bag ready for the morning
- dusting off and re charging your work laptop or mobile phone, if you have one

2) Re read your re-integration support plan

If you have agreed a re-integration plan with your manager then your first day back should be something that holds far less uncertainty. You will already have discussed the measures that will be in place to support you and no doubt your colleagues will be looking forward to seeing you again. You may already have a schedule for the first few days so you know exactly what to expect.

3) Stay positive

Staying positive is so much easier when you have a plan and when you have supportive people around you. Decide in your own mind that you are just going to do your best and learn as you go. Trust me, it will be absolutely fine.

Helping yourself in the future

1. Household chores

A friend of mine once shared with me a wonderful saying from her grandmother:

> "A visitor who notices dust in your house is not worth knowing as a friend."

How true – yet how much we worry ourselves about it! During your return to work, and for a long time beyond that, keeping your home spick and span will be like pushing water uphill. Just thinking about it will make you feel (even more) tired and you know it will be a waste of time before you start. In those first few weeks, be kind to yourself. It is not a disaster if the household chores pile up. You will get to them at some point and it will get easier.

Once you are back at work and have more money coming in you might want to think about hiring a cleaner and / or someone to do the ironing. This can be an enormous support to a busy working mum. If this is an option that you can afford then do give it serious consideration, unless you enjoy cleaning and ironing! If it is not an option then sharing the chores is another way of reducing your home based workload. I recognise that in many homes women still do most of the housework, even if they also have a job, but a refreshing number of women have shared with me that their husband does all the family ironing as part of supporting the family team. Perhaps times are beginning to change.

Household chores featured in another support planning session I held with a particularly focused mum. She decided to create a chart for her fridge door so she could assign the morning jobs between her and her husband. It listed who would empty the dishwasher, hang any damp clothes out to dry as well as who would put the bins out for the bin men. Whether this approach worked in her home or not I don't know but it would certainly have enlightened her husband as to the number of invisible chores she was doing that made the house tick and make it clear that she expected him to help.

2) Making 'me time' a priority

Re-charging your own batteries is usually way down the list of priorities but we are surrounded by mobile phones, laptops and bluetooth devices that regularly need re-charging and you need to re-charge too. The whole family sees the benefit afterwards so it creates a virtuous cycle. It doesn't need to take much time or be planned in detail for it to be effective. Perhaps escaping to the gym is what you need. Perhaps the perfect alone time might be at the nearest mall getting some retail therapy or having the opportunity to get a massage or a facial. A cup of tea and a cake with a friend is popular too. Having an hour for yourself when you can snuggle into a soft dressing gown, slap on a facemask and paint your toenails whilst listening to your favourite music can be all it takes to give you a lift. However you re-charge your batteries building 'me time' into those first few weeks will be hugely beneficial. If you want this to happen I recommend that you write it down on your calendar as you would a commitment to meet a friend. You wouldn't let her down last minute and this way you are more likely to keep your date with yourself.

Enlisting the help of friends and family

If you are blessed with helpful family and friends then do accept their offers of help during your first few weeks back at work. This phase in your life is akin to bringing your baby home from hospital after the birth. You will be tired as your new routine beds in and it is likely that you will have a lot to get your head around as you start to immerse yourself back into work. Any help you can get to lighten the load is a good thing. Family and friends will know that you are about to go back to work and will want to help. Showing them your home support plan will help them to see how they might be a part of it. Offers can vary from one off favours to more regular assistance. The few examples below might trigger your own thoughts:

- Taking the dog for a walk for you
- Looking after the baby while you get out or flake out for an hour!
- Just being there for a supportive chat on the phone those first few nights

There are infinite ways in which family and friends can help. Surrounding yourself with positive people who have confidence in you and encourage you as you become a working mum is vital. If you have friends or family who you know tend to be pessimistic or negative then don't involve them in this plan and definitely don't call them when you are tired. The people you choose need to be uplifting and if people such as these know their role in supporting you, you will feel the benefit.

Involving your husband / partner and pets!

Whenever I use this home support framework I suggest that women talk specifically to their husband or partner and share both their work and home based support plans.

We know that men like to solve problems but are not necessarily comfortable when it comes to listening sympathetically about our feelings. Showing your husband or partner your home support plan demonstrates that you already have the framework for a solution and plays to his natural problem solving strengths. It allows him the opportunity to come up with suggestions of his own as to how he might help and see that there are areas where you really do need him to step in to do certain things that he may not have done in the past. This advice obviously applies equally if you are part of a same sex couple. Whatever your family situation you will probably find that your relationship with your other half changes somewhat once you go back to work. Having an open chat beforehand about who will do what around the home is valuable.

While I was working with one woman on her home support plan she realised that her husband was due to be away during her first week back at work. She quickly realised that camping on a local hillside helping the boy scouts to achieve their camping badge was not where she needed him to be that week and made a note to talk to him that evening about being at home with her instead. He changed his plans.

Another woman realised the need for her husband to have a support plan because he was going to be responsible for the nursery run in the mornings. She wanted to share the design of a support plan with him so it could accommodate his needs too. She was especially keen for him to talk with his employer about a later start time in the first week to reduce his stress levels.

"Remember to cuddle the dog" featured in a recent support plan where a mum worried that, in the frenzy of activity, the family pooch might feel forgotten. Perhaps "cuddle my significant other" might feature somewhere too!

Summary of Part 4

When a well constructed Re-integration Support Proposal is combined with a helpful Home Support Plan something changes for a mum who is about to go back to work. She suddenly feels understood, valued, organised and mentally prepared for what lies ahead.

Part 4 provided two recipes or frameworks to enable you to enlist the help of others in a co-ordinated and personally tailored way. The main message to get across is that returning to work after maternity leave, especially if it is your first baby, is a major life change. You don't have to do everything yourself as you become a working mum so don't try to be super woman.

- Ask for support at work and you'll be pleasantly surprised at how ready your employer will be to meet your requests.
- Say 'Yes' to offers of help at home and channel that help where you need it most.
- Be kind to yourself and make time to recharge or just do nothing at all.

Hopefully this section has sparked some ideas of your own that will make a real difference to you, your employer and your family in those first few weeks and months.

For many of you this will be the last part of this book that you will need to read as you prepare to go back to work. If you are happy to close the book at this point and feel you have gained what you needed from it then may I refer you to the end of the book for Closing Words of Encouragement.

For those of you who wish to read on, Part 5 addresses the scenario that you receive a 'No' from your employer to your part-time working request and helps you to assess your options. Part 5 also recognises that, as time goes by, you can face challenges or changes both at home and at work that mean your part-time working pattern needs a re-think. For those who wish to read on let's take a look at Part 5 and the inspiring interviews that demonstrate how you can adapt to preserve your work / family balance.

PART 5

How do I stay on track when
I go back?

Leaves falling onto the line is normal!

The purpose of this book has always been to empower you as you navigate your way to a happy working pattern, one that enables you to give of your best at work and be the mum you want to be at home. While some of you will arrive at your optimum arrangement first time others may find it takes more than one attempt and this is where this section will help. Many of the mums I interviewed spoke of needing to make amendments or tweaks to their working arrangements after they had gone back to work. So if, in a few months time, you find you slot into this category too then don't worry, yet again you are not alone and there are solutions.

There seem to be three main reasons why a return to work can veer off track.

- You receive a 'No' to your initial part-time working request.

- From the very start your agreed part-time working pattern just doesn't deliver the benefits that you and / or your manager thought it would.

- Your agreed part-time working pattern is a success to start with but circumstances change over time (either at work or at home) and it no longer delivers the benefits that it used to.

Three mums share how they got back on track

In this section I have included three interviews with mums who have been through rather bumpy journeys to find the working pattern that allows them to give of their best both at work and at home. Despite the hurdles they faced they pursued the working pattern that they were convinced was right for them.

As with the first set of interviews I have included a chart so you can see an overview of each interview beforehand.

Name	Role	Company	Detail
Cerys	Head of Department	Secondary School	Part-time working requests refused twice. Resigned to work part-time as a teacher elsewhere.
Emma	Management Accountant	Financial Services Sector	Original return to work solution did not deliver expected benefits. Changed job and employer.
Toni	Researcher	University Hospital	Changes and challenges at work and at home led to a total change of career.

My employer said 'No'! What do I do now?

A large majority of part-time working requests are agreed by employers, which is great news, but what happens to the mums who are told 'No'? While this book is designed to help you get a resounding 'Yes' it would be incomplete without advice and encouragement for those of you who find that, despite your best efforts, your request is refused.

The first thing to recognize is that 'No' doesn't always mean what you think it means, so don't lose hope of finding a solution that works with your current employer. If this happens you may be very disappointed but don't assume the worst and don't give up. You don't know what might have been going on in your workplace that might have led your employer to reach this decision. You don't know if they have something else in mind to discuss with you that has only recently emerged as an option. Stay positive and keep communicating until you understand exactly what the 'No' means. Your employer will invite you to a meeting to explain their decision and this will give you the chance to explore whether there are any other opportunities.

If your company can see no way of taking you back on a flexible basis and insist that your only option is to go back on your old full-time terms then keep the letter they have sent to you so you can be clear on the reasons why this is the case and think very carefully about your options. This type of 'No' represents a crossroads and your options usually are:

- Go back under your previous terms and conditions and wait 12 months to re submit another flexible working request for part-time working.

- Go back under your previous terms and conditions and actively look for other job opportunities internally and externally that are a better fit with your part-time aspirations.

- Go back under your previous terms and conditions and appeal internally following your company's procedures. Do be aware that an appeal is not necessarily going to change anything. Your manager's decision is likely to be backed up by the company. An appeal usually looks at whether the process has been followed properly. It does not usually assess whether the decision should be re examined. A copy of the appeals process should be available from your HR team.

- Take your employer to an Employment Tribunal. Again a tribunal will only look at whether the correct process was followed rather than reassess your employer's decision. Figures from HM Courts and Tribunal service show that in 2010-2011 over 218,000 tribunal claims were made and only 277 claims were related to flexible working applications. Most of these flexible working related claims were settled outside of a tribunal via ACAS (Advisory, Conciliation and Arbitration Service). Of the 48 claims that went through to tribunal only 10 were successful. Please give serious consideration as to whether you want to expend the energy required to go through this process.

- Resign. If you do this you will not be expected to go back into the office to work your notice period and you are entitled to be paid for the holiday you have accrued during your maternity leave. Note that depending upon your company's maternity policy you may be required to re pay any maternity pay you have received that was over and above Statutory Maternity Pay. If so then this should be very clearly stated in your company maternity policy and therefore not be a surprise. In any event you will not be expected to re pay Statutory Maternity Pay.

Only you can decide in which direction you want to go after a 'No'. Resigning and embracing a new start somewhere else that does meet your needs as a parent is going to feel a bit scary. Stepping into the unknown will always feel unsettling but there is life and work beyond your current company. Whichever option you choose it is in your best interests to stay on good terms with your employer especially if you want a positive reference at some point in the future.

When I initially received my 'No' letter I was devastated. I opened the letter while sat in my car in a supermarket car park with my baby daughter prior to doing the weekly shop. It felt as though I had been rejected. I knew there and then that going back full-time was something I absolutely did not want to do. I had no idea what the next steps were or what my options could be and I felt totally lost. A few days later I received a text from the colleague covering my maternity leave saying that she had just resigned as she had found a better paid job closer to home. I remember feeling really glad for her and wondered what difference that might make for me. Shortly after I received a call from my manager asking me to come into the office to discuss alternative options beyond my flexible working request and from there we reached a solution that worked for both parties and I agreed to a trial period. To this day I am glad that I had the opportunity to go back to work, however that opportunity might have come about.

So a 'No' may not be the final word and arranging a meeting as soon as possible to understand exactly what it does mean and what your employer sees as your options will certainly be worthwhile. The interview that follows shows how one mum handled a 'No' decision from her employer.

Introduction to Cerys, Secondary School Teacher

Cerys went into teaching after graduating and has now been a secondary school teacher for 15 years. At the point that she became pregnant with her first child she had reached the level of Head of Department. Cerys' regular income is vital to her family as her husband is self employed and his income fluctuates. Cerys twice received a 'No' to part-time working from her employer and although she returned to work on a full-time basis both times she found the demands of full-time work, while raising two boys under the age of 4, was too much. This led her to resign and find a part-time teaching role in a different school, where she is far happier.

Where was your career at the point at which you started your first maternity leave?

I'd been teaching for 11 years and I was Head of a French department in a secondary school, so I was in a middle management role.

For the benefit of those who don't work in teaching can you explain what responsibility comes with that role?

Ok, so I was responsible for the teaching staff, the language assistants and part-time staff. My role involved raising standards in the department, making sure staff were performing and teaching classes myself of course. I'd teach up to GCSE and A Level as Head of Department.

What were your working hours at that time?

Well officially I was in work from 8.30am to 3.30pm five days a week and then there would be plenty of work to do at home and on weekends, marking, planning, admin, anything to do with running the department.

How long were you on maternity leave for?

I took 6 months because that's how long I could take and still get some sort of pay. I went back to work just before the end of the summer term and I worked a week and a half so that I was back in employment before the start of the summer holidays. That meant that I got paid during the summer holidays. By that time I was very low on money and if I hadn't gone back to work for that week I would have had to survive the summer with no pay at all.

It sounds as though going back to work was very much driven by a financial motive.

Very much so! I was then and I am now the main earner. There is more responsibility on me or pressure on me because my wage is constant whereas my husband's wage is not guaranteed and can fluctuate every month because Dafydd is self employed.

So you contacted your employer in order to go back. Did you request any changes to your hours or role when you went back?

Well at that time I didn't think about it you know, I was glad I had a job and I just accepted that the work I had been doing in the evenings would still need to be done and it would be quite hard to do that with a baby as well. I suppose at the time I thought I could juggle it all but it didn't quite work out like that. In teaching, whatever you decide to do when you go back, be it part-time or full-time, there is no sort of easing in period. In my experience there was no support, I was straight back in. I remember that when I went back I had a meeting beforehand on the Friday with my Head he said,

"X is doing this, Y is doing that and you need to sort it out."

There was no recognition that I'd been away for 6 months and been out of the loop.

I guess it comes down to your line manager and their empathy and understanding. If they have some towards you then it goes such a long way and if there is no understanding at all it can make the return very hard.

Yes, there was very little contact, if any, from senior management in that school. But it does depend on who you are working with.

So you didn't do any negotiation on your return to work after your first baby because you went back to the same job, full-time. When you had your second baby did you decide to go back full-time then as well and keep juggling everything?

No, I did ask to go back part-time after I had my second son, Rhodri. I wanted to work four days a week instead of five. I actually asked twice to be able to work four days a week and I was turned down both times. The first time they told me I'd applied too late before the start of the academic year and the second time I applied they just said 'No'. So I got to the stage where I thought something has got to give here because there was just too much pressure really. So for my health, for my family, I recently resigned. I thought that financially I'll find something else and we will manage but I can't keep doing this. And now I've done it, it feels like the best decision.

Why do you think your employer turned down your requests to work part-time?

Looking back now, I think maybe they just couldn't accommodate the changes they would have had to make to my timetable. By then my colleague and I, who were teaching in the same department, were also teaching another subject other than our own. If my teaching hours were cut there would have been no one else to soak up my hours. I needed more empathy from my boss and I needed to have some pressure taken off me. It was a really tough time and I felt as if I'd reached a dead end. I didn't feel like a valued member of the team.

So how is the part-time job hunting going?

Well I've already got a new job in a different local secondary school ready for the next academic year. It's a 12 month contract so I'll have to re apply next year or look for something different. If it all goes well I'm hoping I'll be taken on permanently as a part-time member of staff.

That's great, congratulations! Tell me about your new role what are you going to be doing?

Ok, so in September I'll be working in a different school on 0.5 which basically means half the timetable. It doesn't conveniently fit into 2.5 days a week because my teaching time is spread throughout the week but I do get one full working day every week. I'm no longer Head of Department so I won't have any responsibility for teaching GCSE or A level classes. I'm teaching year 7 to 9. Basically all I have to do is go in and teach and be a teacher and won't have to worry about targets or development plans. I just have to look after my little patch if you like. And I'm really looking forward to it. It will be much better. I'm actually looking forward to going to work!

What difference is that going to make to your morning routine?

It will still mean an early start but it will be more like 6.00am rather than 5.00am. Most mornings I won't need to start work until 10.00am but I will still need to get the boys over to either my mother or the childminder and Ifan starts primary school in September so there is no sort of relaxed start to the day. We will still need to be out of the house by about 8.00am, which is fine because that leaves me a little bit of time then, once I've dropped them off, to maybe do something for myself or get to work at a leisurely pace. I'll usually be finishing work earlier which will be great. I'll be able to collect Ifan from school, maybe do a little bit of shopping.

Was helping Ifan as he started primary school a factor in your desire to work part-time?

Yes, I really wanted to be there for him and I'll be able to drop him off and pick him up now which, with the old job, I wouldn't have been able to do.

You sound really enthusiastic about this new career direction.

Yes, I'm really looking forward to it! I think it will be better for me and better for the boys because I'll have more time for them. I won't be so stressed out. I can be nicer with them if you know what I mean.

Is there anything that in hindsight that you would do differently?

Yes, I'd have applied earlier to go part-time. When I went back to work the first time I thought I could go back full-time and manage my baby as well. It didn't really strike me at the time but I remember people were surprised when I told them I was going back full-time.

Do you have any advice to pass on to other mums who receive a 'No' to their part-time working request?

There is always a way to make your life easier. If you can't make enough tweaks whilst working full-time, then it might be time to become braver and look for other options. It's a massive step and a huge risk to take for some of us, but if something's making you unhappy, it's worth the risk. I definitely don't regret the decision I made.

Key Points from Cerys' interview

1) Avoiding workload overload

An overwhelming workload was a big factor in Cerys' decision to leave her full-time job and search for part-time work. The part-time role she secured has given her the time she wanted to spend with her two boys and, despite a drop in income, her quality of life feels better as a result.

Workload is such an important point to come from Cerys' interview because it is easy to assume that, once you have secured your part-time role, your workload will be entirely manageable. Workload creeping up over time is a factor that many part-time workers need to keep an eye on. In virtually every interview I have conducted mums returning from maternity leave have felt very grateful toward their employer for allowing them to go back on part-time terms and want to give something back in return to show their commitment. This is even more applicable in a recessionary environment with the inherent pressures to go the extra mile. However there are limits to the extra that a part-time employee can offer. In reality you have two jobs and your role as mum starts as soon as you leave your workplace and it is just as demanding, if not more demanding.

Another contributor to this book, Hannah, told me how she had left a well paid job as a surveyor after her workload crept up to an unmanageable level. Hannah negotiated well for a part-time role working 3 days a week but 18 months after she returned to work she found she was working almost full-time hours for part-time pay. The balance she had negotiated so hard for after maternity leave had been eroded over time until she felt tired, disgruntled and taken for granted.

If, at some point in the future, you find yourself in this situation then I would certainly recommend talking to your employer long before you reach breaking point. A good employer will recognise that more has been placed on you than is reasonable within your contracted hours and make adjustments to reduce hours and stress. In reality your manager may need some time to respond and adjust the situation so for this reason it is important not to suffer in silence. What happens beyond that conversation can only be positive if you stay committed to finding the balance you want to achieve.

<u>Where is Cerys now?</u>

Cerys is still working at the new school and has just been taken on as a permanent part-time member of the teaching staff. She continues to work a 0.5 timetable and benefits from the extra time she has at home with her boys. Despite the drop in income her new working pattern is providing the balance she was looking for and she is far happier.

From the very start my part-time working pattern has just not worked the way I thought it would!

My own return to work, once it was agreed, definitely qualifies for this 'just not working the way I thought it would' category! When I went back to work I returned to the same role and worked Monday to Friday on reduced hours, 9.00am to 3.00pm, with no lunch break.

In designing my part-time working pattern I had not asked about or considered the changes that had occurred in both the business and my role while I'd been away. Three main factors meant my part-time working pattern was sure to fail from the start.

- The foreign business travel required to meet the demands of my role had increased dramatically during my maternity leave. This was not something I could easily accommodate as my husband's job required him to travel internationally every week and he is the main earner in our family. Added to this my parents live too far away to help with overnight childcare.

- My team were unable to pick up many of the responsibilities I had identified for re-assignment because they were stretched to capacity implementing an explosion of new product related projects.

- I had not given thought to the true drop in hours that my new working pattern represented. Before my daughter was born I would work a 10 hour day most days. To suddenly drop from approximately 50 hours a week to 30 hours without relinquishing any part of the role was never going to be a success.

As a result I spent an increasing amount of my evenings working over time at home and negotiating with my husband about how we could each meet our business travel responsibilities. I didn't investigate what had changed in my workplace when I designed my part-time working pattern and as a result I didn't get the benefits from working part-time that I had expected.

Emma's interview below shows that I was not alone in designing a return to work solution that, when put into practice, did not bring the benefits that were expected. Emma made some major changes to arrive at a happy solution.

Introduction to Emma, Management Accountant.

Emma is married to Mark and they have one son, Daniel. When Emma fell pregnant she was working full-time as a management accountant in the financial services sector. As the main earner in her family Emma's income is vital. This created a level of pressure in itself but added to that Emma was unhappy in her role before she fell pregnant and, as a result, she was dreading going back to work after maternity leave.

Negotiations with her manager meant that she returned to work on a compressed hours working pattern i.e. she would work the hours associated with a 5 day week over 4 days, Monday to Thursday, and then have Friday off. For a number of reasons this didn't work for her.

The interview covers Emma's initial return to work on compressed hours with the employer where she was unhappy and then her move to her new employer where she is far happier and works 5 days a week with flexibility to work from home when needed.

Emma, would you set the scene for me and explain a bit about your job at the point at which you started your maternity leave?

My employer at that time had just merged with another company so there was a lot of change in the office. My career was doing alright but I wasn't too enthusiastic about it. I worked full-time and was probably 1 year away from a next step. I was working Monday to Friday 9.00am to 5.00pm. There was a little bit of travel required with my role, just going from Bristol to London one day a week. The commute into Bristol everyday was a bit painful because it could take anything from 40 minutes to 1 hour 30 minutes.

What did you enjoy about your job at that point?

I can't remember really. I wasn't very happy at work to be honest. I was a bit bored both on the job front and colleague wise too. I'm a very sociable person and the culture of my department didn't really suit me. My previous role was in a large insurance company and had required lots of travel. I was on the road 4 days a week covering the UK and Ireland and I absolutely loved that. I enjoyed the variety and seeing the countryside. But I'd done that for two years when my role was made redundant and that was probably enough. I wouldn't want to do that now. So to answer your question, my first experience of working in a big head office coincided with my pregnancy and I wasn't really enjoying my job.

How old was Daniel when you went back to work?

He was 9 months old when I went back. I had always planned to go back after 9 months because that's how long my husband and I could survive without my pay. My husband is self employed and I am the main earner with a regular salary.

So were your reasons for going back to work purely financial?

I'd say they were primarily financial but I do enjoy work and I get a lot out of it. I'm not proud though and given the choice

I'd happily stay at home with Daniel. It wouldn't bother me at all. If I had the money and didn't have to work full-time then I wouldn't work full-time. I'd do something though, preferably from home, to keep my brain ticking over.

When did you start planning your return to work?

I went back to work in the March so I probably started planning my return a few months before that around Christmastime. I used Keep In Touch days to ease my way back into the office. The reason I did KIT days was purely financial because my employer paid me my normal salary for each day that I worked, so again, if I hadn't needed to do them I probably wouldn't have done them. But I had to go back to work in March.

My planning involved talking with my boss and arranging the dates for the KIT days and once they were agreed and I knew I was going to be paid for them I worked out that financially I could extend my maternity leave and go back at the end of March, which gave me almost another month with Daniel.

How did you decide upon a compressed hours working pattern?

I discussed it with my husband, Mark, and we agreed that we didn't want Daniel in a nursery 5 days a week from such an early age. We thought it was too much for him and that if I had a day off on Friday and Mark had a day off on Monday then Daniel would only be in nursery 3 days a week. So I asked my boss if I could go back on a compressed week. That meant working 35 hours in 4 days.

From a commuting perspective it worked really well. I was in work by 7.30am and I missed all the traffic. I'd leave by 5.30pm and get home by 6.30pm but I didn't really see Daniel awake at all during those 4 days. In the end I don't think I could have sustained that long term. Maybe without the travel at either end of my day it may have worked but I'd probably have had to go back to 5 days a week, 9.00am to 5.00pm, just to see Daniel.

When did you realise that working the compressed week would mean not seeing Daniel awake for 4 days a week?

I always envisaged that that's what it would mean but I thought that being with him for 3 days would balance it out. I probably didn't realise how tired I'd be but then, going back to work, I'd have been tired anyway. The only thing that became a dawning realisation was the fact that, during the 4 days a week that I worked, the childcare was entirely down to my husband. So although I was around for 3 days I was out of the picture for 4 days. So I think that was another thing that killed it as a working arrangement.

Was your manager open to the idea of you working a compressed week?

No, my manager wasn't normally in favour of compressed weeks but he'd rather accommodate me rather than lose me.

So you rightly anticipated that working a compressed week would give the best childcare balance for Daniel and it would work financially too.

Yes and these were benefits that we definitely got from that arrangement.

But there were unexpected disadvantages?

Yes. I knew that I wouldn't see Daniel much during my 4 working days but I didn't expect that I would miss him so much. I knew I'd be tired but I was really very tired and the responsibility for childcare during those 4 days was not evenly balanced at home.

Plus you said you were not terribly happy in the job anyway.

No, I wasn't and I started looking for another job about two months before I went back to work. So in the January I started looking around. I wanted to stay in financial services but find an employer nearer to home. I had a company in mind and I looked on their website and saw there were jobs to apply for via their website. So that's what I did. I didn't get involved with agencies. I applied on-line, filled out the application and attached my CV, which didn't take much thinking about because I'd already prepared it before my maternity leave started. Things happened really fast because I got a call on the Friday to say my interview was on the Monday!

They were sending me through details of a presentation that I had to prepare and they were also sending me a link to do on-line aptitude tests in Maths and English. That was really focussing! All of a sudden I had to remember what I did in my previous roles, prepare for the presentation and do the Maths and English test. That was when I dived into getting my brain working again. I was in at the deep end and I didn't know how I'd do. Obviously I did alright because they offered me the job.

I remember in the interview they were asking things like,

"Give me an example of when you've done this or shown teamwork."

I was really struggling for examples from my role at that time so I gave examples from my previous role at the insurance company instead. The truth was that I couldn't remember what I did anymore in my job!

Do you think your answers referring to your previous role came more readily because you enjoyed that job more?

Probably, yes! I was more enthusiastic in that job and more proud of what I'd done. I told my interviewer that I couldn't discuss my current role for reasons of confidentiality and I think she was happy with that.

So you recognised that you were going back to a job where you weren't too happy and you applied for a new job while you were on maternity leave?

Yes, the thought of going back to work didn't worry me because I always knew I'd have to but the thought of going back to a job that I hated really did worry me.

Did you look into whether your employer would respond to your resignation by asking you to pay back any maternity pay you'd had in addition to Statutory Maternity Pay?

Yes, I looked into all that and there was no requirement for me to re pay my maternity pay.

That's good! Talk me through how you went back to work and then resigned.

Well I wanted to tell my boss face to face while I was working my Keep In Touch days but it took so long for my new employer to send my new contract through that I ended up telling him on my first proper day back in the office. I felt a bit wrong doing that but I couldn't prolong it. Even worse – my boss was not in the office that week, he was in London! So I had to do it over the phone, but he was fine about it.

How much notice did you have to work?

1 month.

And you worked your notice on compressed hours?

Yes, I thought they might have let me take it a bit easy but they got me involved in a load of big projects. I ended up doing a lot of work in that month.

What hours are you working now in your new role?

I'm contracted to do a 35 hour week from Monday to Friday but I probably do a sustained 40 to 45 hour week. At the start I probably did a few 50 hour weeks and I was astonished when I realised! I never thought I'd work a 50 hour week in my life but I enjoy my work now and it's busy in the office so the time flies. Although I'm employed full-time my employer allows me to work within a flexible hours working pattern so if I need to be at home I can work from home or make hours up in the evenings.

You are happier in the culture of your new employer?

Yes and my manager is really understanding. If I need to leave early to collect Daniel from nursery then it's not a problem. My boss would never criticise me for doing that because so many employees are in the same situation and the hours get done and the work gets done.

So you achieved a better work / family balance once you started working for the new employer closer to home?

Yes, it's much closer and the roads are better, no motorways and no traffic jams. I'm enjoying the new job a lot more.

Well you are smiling so it must be working, the job, the culture, the hours and the commute!

Yes, basically.

Your move to your new employer meant you stopped working a compressed week but what did you learn from the compressed week experience?

I'm aware that I mustn't let Mark do the majority of the childcare or it will come back to haunt me! Despite discussing upfront the fact that Mark would be the primary carer for Daniel 4 days a week, it still became a bone of contention between us and I'd get complaints when I got home like,

"I've been looking after Daniel all week! Whose job is more important? My job is just as important as yours!"

That is something to really clarify up front and agree with each other. When I'd started back on compressed hours in Bristol Mark quickly felt that it was an unfair arrangement and by then it was too late, we were committed. Thankfully it was only for 4 weeks!

Now I work 5 days a week doing more normal office hours and I'm located much closer to home so that combination of changes has made a real difference. At the start of every week I can arrange with Mark whether I am doing the nursery pick up all week or the nursery drop off. Another huge help is my employer's willingness to allow me to work from home occasionally when I need to juggle work and family.

The last question is what advice would you pass on to other mums whose original part-time working pattern is not delivering the benefits they expected?

The only advice I would give is to be upfront with your employer. If you are unhappy about the situation then work with them to understand the other options that might be available to you. Trial other options until you find something that works for you and your employer. Do be realistic though. Don't expect any arrangement to be easy. It's always a juggling act!

Overall I think my new working pattern is a success for me because it allows me to juggle my home and work responsibilities and respond to situations as they arise. I also have the support of my husband or parents whenever I need to work late and that has been fundamental.

Key Points from Emma's interview

Emma's experience shows how even intelligent, professional women can ask for a part-time working pattern that simply doesn't work the way they envisaged! Despite this failed first attempt Emma continued to proactively pursue a happy solution. Taking action to secure a more enjoyable role that was also closer to her home had a significant and beneficial impact on both her and her family. There are a number of other points that are worth noting.

1) Brush up your CV as maternity leave starts

It is always a good idea to have your CV up to date regardless of where you are in your career and doing this as you start your maternity leave is really worthwhile. You will write a far better CV while you can remember what your job involved and you feel connected to your work identity. If it turns out later on that you need your CV – you are prepared straight away. If you don't need it then reading it later will help you to reconnect with your achievements as you prepare to go back to work. The simple act of reacquainting yourself with your past achievements will be a positive experience.

2) Talk with your employer before you walk away

While changing employer was the right decision for Emma she herself emphasises the importance of talking to your employer before walking away. Do discuss your situation with your manager to see if there are changes that can be made to your working pattern that will resolve the issues you are facing.

I did exactly that when my original part-time working pattern proved to be wrong for the role. I had a very honest meeting with my manager where I explained that even though I was doing significant hours at home I still did not feel on top of the job. Unbeknownst to me the foreign travel had increased during my absence and I could not ask my husband to continually reschedule his work around mine. I said that I was happy to consider other roles and appreciated that it may take me time to resolve the situation so I would give it another 6 months. If I could not find anything suitable in the company in that time then I would resign. My boss was very understanding and 3 months later he offered me another role, without foreign travel. I gave this new role a 6 month trial but I had a miscarriage during that time and it led me to re-think my career. I resigned "to pursue other interests" i.e. retrain and write a book!

What my experience shows is that once you are back in the workplace and proving your worth once again your manager is likely to want to keep you. Please give your company a chance and talk before you walk away!

3) Changing employer during maternity leave

Returning to work after maternity leave is so much easier if you:

- work for a boss you get on well with
- have a job you enjoy and
- work in a company where you feel you belong.

If this does not apply to you and you are really worried about going back to a job or company where you are unhappy then it is possible to find another job, with a different employer, whilst on maternity leave. We will look at changing role, employer and even career in more detail after the next interview with Toni.

4) Check any requirement to re pay maternity pay if you decide to resign

If you do decide to apply for a different job whilst on maternity leave do check that your current employer does not expect you to re pay any maternity pay that they have given you that is in addition to Statutory Maternity Pay (SMP). If this is the case then it should be very clearly stated in your company maternity policy. You will not have to re pay any SMP you have received.

5) Keep talking at home about how it is working out

Emma mentioned the friction that her original part-time working pattern caused between her and her husband. Do assess the pros and cons of your chosen working pattern with your family beforehand. Be honest about what the disadvantages may be for everyone and agree how you will address them. Once you are back at work keep talking at home about the pros and cons. Are they what you expected or are they different? Are they more severe than you expected or not so impactful? Has your plan to work around any challenges been effective? As you become a working mum for the first time it is unrealistic to expect to get everything right first time but if you keep identifying the challenges and try new ways to remove or reduce their impact you will find a solution that works.

<u>Where is Emma now?</u>

Emma still works full-time flexible hours for her new employer and enjoys both her work and her working environment. She is able to work from home on those occasions when it is needed. Emma has been promoted twice since joining the company and now holds a Senior Finance Manager role.

My part-time arrangement worked well initially but it's not working at all now!

We are surrounded by change both at home and at work. As our children grow they gradually become more independent and what they require from us in terms of support alters. Change in the workplace is constant and only those individuals and businesses that can adapt successfully will thrive. It shouldn't come as a shock then that a part-time working agreement will require tweaks, alterations and refinements over time too.

If the changes in the workplace or home are small then a minor tweak to your part-time working arrangement can be all that is required, such as the changes made by Julie, Helen and Suzy in their interviews in Part 2;

- Julie found staying later on a Friday to finish things off before the weekend enabled her to switch off and know her In Tray was under control.

- Helen changed her 3 working days from Tuesday, Wednesday, and Thursday in her initial project management role to Monday, Wednesday, and Thursday to reflect the needs of her subsequent operational project role.

- Suzy swapped her Tuesday late shift for a Tuesday day shift in order to help accommodate her husband's business travel.

If the changes in the home or workplace are major then it can require a correspondingly big re-think of working pattern, role, employer or even career. The interview that follows with Toni highlights some of the personal and professional changes that can lead mums to seek a totally different path.

Introduction to Toni, Medical Researcher

Toni is a PhD Medical Researcher. She was employed full-time as a Research Associate in a large University hospital when she fell pregnant with her first child. She returned to work on a part-time basis after 9 months of maternity leave and her son, Bryson, went to a local nursery from Monday to Thursday. After 2 years back at work a number of challenges and changes, both at home and at work, coincided;

- *dissatisfaction with career progress*
- *the looming possibility of redundancy*
- *a suspicion that all was not right with Bryson*
- *becoming pregnant for the second time*

This meant that a big re-think was necessary:

The convergence of all these factors makes Toni's story rather extreme and it is highly unlikely that you will experience the same number of challenges simultaneously. This interview demonstrates how a difficult situation can be a catalyst to finding a better work / family balance.

Where was your career at the point at which you started your first maternity leave?

I was working as a Medical Research Associate. My manager was both a Clinical Consultant in a hospital and a Professor in a university leading a number of research teams working on different projects. My role was quite independent and my project was funded externally. The start of my maternity leave loosely coincided with the end of the funding, which meant in theory I had nothing to go back to. Whilst I was on maternity leave I successfully applied for funding to start a new research project in a similar field. So I planned to go back and run this research project myself for the period of the funding, which was two and half years.

How old was Bryson when you went back to work?

He was 8 months old

Were you happy in your new role?

Substantially yes, I enjoyed the work I was doing. Because I had been proactive in applying for research funding whilst I was on maternity leave I was able to shape the project to the hours that I wanted to work. I created a 4 day a week role that required me to be at work Monday to Thursday from 8.00am till 4.45pm. This meant I could easily collect my little one from nursery at the end of the day. Of course there were still occasions when I needed to ask hubby to collect Bryson but it was a workable working pattern.

Problems started to emerge shortly after I went back to work because I was denied a promotion that I felt I was due and was told to wait 12 months to reapply. About 8 months after my return the university changed the promotion structure. It meant that promotion was further out of my reach because I wasn't supervising anyone at that time. The fact that I had supervised staff in the past didn't matter. I couldn't tick the supervisor box there and then so I was not eligible to be re-considered for a re-grade.

That must have been disappointing and frustrating!

Yes! I actually applied for additional funding to pay for an assistant and I got that extra funding! My manager agreed that in order to make the extra money stretch further we should recruit a PhD student to assist me and this would enable me to check the supervisor box for promotion. I assisted in the interviewing for a PhD student but when that person arrived my boss diverted them off to work on another project instead. So I felt very much that I was getting mixed messages and the things that I had been promised were not being put in place. I felt my career wasn't going anywhere, despite all my hard work. I really didn't feel valued at all.

So your part-time working pattern was meeting your needs but there was still a rather unhappy picture developing at work?

Yes

How long were you employed in this working pattern? Was it the duration of that funding?

Yes about two and a half years.

What were the changes or new challenges in work or at home that led you to re think your part-time working pattern?

There were a lot of things both at home and at work.

At work the way I'd been treated in relation to my promotion request had a lasting impact on me but another problem at work was that my boss micro managed me. He always wanted to know exactly what was going on and he would call me at home at about 8.00pm in the evening to talk about what I'd been doing. Of course that clashed with me trying to get my little one off to bed. In addition there was talk of redundancies at work. We were having redundancy meetings and I knew my funding was coming to an end.

At home Bryson had always been hard work especially at bedtime. So my boss calling at 8.00pm was really not appreciated. It just seemed that it would get to 10.00pm everyday and I hadn't stopped! I felt completely shattered. I was on a treadmill. I wasn't spending any quality time with my son, I was just functioning day after day.

At about this time we noticed that Bryson, who was 2 years old by this point, was a bit slow in learning how to talk and he wasn't able to sit still for story time at nursery like the other children. We'd had numerous assessments from people within speech and language services who had gone into nursery to assess Bryson. There were just a couple of things that indicated there might be something else going on with him and although we knew we had a child who was hard work we began to see that he might need more help than we had anticipated.

At about the same time I got pregnant again and I knew my funding was coming to an end at work. Suddenly we had another baby on the way and I was faced with the prospect of writing more funding applications to keep me on a treadmill while all these tests were going on with Bryson plus the possibility of redundancy.

By that point we needed to take some time out from all of it and figure out what would work best for Bryson and us. We needed to re assess. I think it was about this time that I decided in my own mind to take redundancy at work if it was offered. I'd never been through redundancy before but I'd had enough and as a family we needed a re-think.

There was so much happening for you at home against a backdrop of an uncertain and unhappy work situation. That's a lot to hit you all at once. What happened next?

My husband and I discussed the situation. I decided to work through my second pregnancy while the funding lasted, have my maternity leave and then take voluntary redundancy. So by the time Bryson started primary school I was at home full-time. My life was focused on being mum to Samuel and Bryson.

How did Bryson adapt to primary school?

Bryson started primary school on a morning only basis initially and I really didn't think it would be as hard for him to adjust as it was. He'd been at nursery from 8.00am till

5.00pm four days a week and been fine. There had been very few incidents. I expected him, within a couple of weeks, to be at school full-time. It took 8 months. Bryson was about four and a half when he started school and by then he was being assessed both at school and at home. We got the Aspergers diagnosis about six months later when he was five.

For those people who don't know much about Aspergers and autism would you explain a bit about it and Bryson's condition?

Well I guess people don't call it autism so much now, they call it ASD – Autistic Spectrum Disorder – because it is a spectrum of disorders and no child will have the exact same presentation as another. Put simply the brains of children with ASD are wired differently and they perceive the world and process information differently from the norm. Bryson scores particularly low in the part of the spectrum that deals with social interaction and social communication skills.

One way that this is demonstrated in his behaviour is that he has no concept of personal space. He's not cut off the way that some autistic children are. If anything he's in your face, he's very over familiar. He doesn't understand at all. The Aspergers specific diagnosis is often given to those children with ASD who are very dependent on routine. If Bryson's life is not run to a fairly strict schedule he's not entirely sure what is going on or what to expect next, this situation causes him great anxiety. When he is outside his comfort zone we often have what is best described as a toddler melt down. There will be flying fists and screaming and shouting.

I suppose that affects your whole family because you need to provide that routine.

Our lives do run to a fairly sort of regimented routine for his benefit. The main thing is that he needs a fairly structured life. He needs to know exactly where he is. When he first started primary school it was quite common for me to go to collect him from school to find him wrapped up inside a curtain and refusing to come out because there had been too many changes that day. It felt as though I was talking to his teacher everyday about some incident or other.

It must have been a tough time for all of you when he started school.

Yes!

Well you are doing a fantastic job because he is now integrated into a primary school. That's a huge achievement for all of you!

It took eight months to get him settled though!

You've given some valuable detail about Bryson's Aspergers and his behaviour and shared how you have adapted as a family to help him. What about you and your career. What did you see as your options at that time?

Well after Samuel was born I did look at a couple of jobs but with far less responsibility. Rather than look for something as a Research Associate I was looking for a job simply as a Technician so I could go in, do the job and go home. I did get offered a job at The Blood Bank but I'd asked them for a part-time job and what they offered me was a full-time job so I declined the offer. After that I started looking for jobs on an evening basis and I got a job in a bar close to home three evenings a week. I did that job for a year and it got me out of the house plus we didn't have childcare costs to cover because it was an evening job.

I guess the bar job gave you a break from a demanding family life.

Well yes, it really was just a short term thing to get me out of the house. At the time I was collecting Bryson from school every day and there were problems at school most days and the only thing in my life was looking after the baby and dealing with Bryson and all the incidents. I just needed to get away from it and get a change of scenery. While I was doing the bar work I thought about re training. I'd thought about becoming a teacher after I'd done my first degree because someone said at the time that I was very good at explaining things.

Interesting, so the idea of being a teacher was given to you years ago by someone saying you had a natural talent for it?

Yes.

And you are now training to teach chemistry to A level students is that right?

Yes, A level and GCSE students

It was something that I had thought about on and off when I went on maternity leave with Bryson. If I hadn't gotten any funding while I was on maternity leave I might have pursued that earlier – but I did get funding so I went back to research. When it started flagging up that Bryson was going to need more attention I looked at it again. We have a child who doesn't like change. I can't stick him in a summer holiday club through the school summer holidays when he gets older and expect him to get on well. A normal job with full-time hours was just not going to work. A school based job, either as a teacher or a science technician, would mean that he wouldn't need to go into childcare in the summer holidays. That was a big pull toward teaching as a career, although I'm still going to take about an £18K pay cut as and when I get my first teaching position.

Are you comfortable with that?

Yes, because I really can't see us being able to get Bryson settled in a holiday club for 6 weeks every summer. I need to do something that is either term time based or where I can take holiday or a sabbatical in the summer period.

You seem to have absolute clarity that Bryson's needs come first and if you can accommodate those needs and find a way to mould your career around them then that is a better solution for the entire family.

Yes. I always thought that I might like to do teacher training but it's kind of been pushed that way because of home stuff and wanting a better quality of life I guess. My career has to fit with the kids while they are young.

You are nearly at the end of your teacher training now. What was it that kept you going? There must have been some tough times so what is it that spurs you on?

Yes there are still tough times such as when I'm working on lesson prep till midnight every night! It isn't easy but what spurs me on is the knowledge that at some point in the future both Bryson and Samuel will be settled in school. Then what am I going to do? I've never been good at sitting around at home. I'm probably the worst housewife in the world! I need to do something with my brain because otherwise I'm bored and miserable. Being a stay at home mum is a nice idea but it is not a good financial choice for us as a family. We can manage at the moment while I'm training but our lives would have a few more luxuries and be a little more fun if I were working and earning.

Once I've qualified I could work from home as a private tutor or I could look at going down different avenues. I'm interested in going into special needs teaching but I think that is partly because when I go into a school as part of my own training I can spot the children who are like Bryson and I know the best way to deal with them. I certainly need to finish my training but I'm not sure that being a full-time teacher at the end of it is the route I want to go. I may eventually go into special needs teaching but do private tutoring from home while the kids are young.

It sounds as though, as you complete your teacher training, you don't have a pre defined working pattern in mind. You are open to the options that this training could provide. It sounds as though your main goal is to find a career that allows you to be there for Bryson.

Yes.

Is completing this training is bringing benefits for you too?

Yes. I'll have an identity rather than just being someone's mum. When your children are little you are just someone's mum and that's how people refer to you, unless you have some kind of work type environment where you go to do something different. That loss of identity is very difficult when you have kids.

How did you feel as you went through the transition from employment through redundancy to teacher training?

I think that through all of this the scariest part was going through the redundancy process, waiting to be made redundant and becoming unemployed. I've always worked full-time and suddenly thinking that I was going to be out of work really worried me. I'd have thoughts like;

"We are going to be on one income! We are not going to be able to manage! What am I going to do? I'm not going to have any goals in life! I'm going to sit around on the sofa and be a Jeremy Kyle person!"

That was a really scary prospect. But the actual reality of being at home and not working and training for something else is ok. Once I learned to relax about not being in work I was fine. I hadn't been out of work since I was 17. The thought of taking myself out of work was the scariest thing. You think;

"I'll never be employed again!"

I think many people going through redundancy for the first time have the same concerns. I certainly did when it happened to me! You mentioned feeling scared of the next step beyond redundancy. Tell me a bit more about that.

The reality of changing course is not as scary as the thought. I don't think I've been without a plan since I was 16.

Since GCSE level I've always been choosing my path and there was a structure and a plan and I knew roughly where I was going. This was the first time in my life where I thought;

"You know, actually, my plan is no good anymore. I need a new plan."

Most kids take time out at around 18 years old to think because that's when they don't know what they want to do. They seem to wander off and go to college or find a job but suddenly I was 34 years old without a plan. No income, no job and no plan! Actually not having a plan was the scariest bit. I thought;

"I'll have to go and work in Woolworths!"

And that doesn't even exist anymore! What advice would you pass on to another mum who has found that she needs to re-think her working pattern or career because of significant changes either at work or at home or both?

Don't panic, take some time out, relax and do what you need to do and figure it all out later. You don't need to have the answers in the beginning because you don't have the answers in the beginning.

It's important to take the time you need to find a solution that will work for all of you?

Yes, but that doesn't mean that my new plan is going to work. I may need to revisit it again in 5 years time! But I'm less stressed about it now. I'm less panicked about it.

You just have to adapt and keep adapting?

Yes, this is our plan for now and if we need to re-think it in future, then we will.

Key Points from Toni's interview

1) Manager expectations about the 'extra mile'.

Toni's manager expected her to be available for work related conversations well outside of her normal working hours and regularly rang her at 8.00pm to catch up. We all know how inconvenient a telephone call during the bedtime routine can be, even when the caller is someone we want to talk to! Most managers will realise that your ability to go the extra mile will have changed since having a baby but unless you discuss exactly what that means they may be left wondering and make incorrect assumptions about thing such as:

- your availability to work overtime
- how regularly you will check emails and phone messages out of hours.

If you find your manager's assumptions in these areas become a problem then do discuss it. The likelihood is that he or she is simply unaware of the intrusion or pressure it is creating. Being clear how far you are able to flex in these areas will be helpful for all concerned.

2) Pay, recognition and responsibility

Let's be honest, we all grumble about not feeling valued or appropriately rewarded from time to time but there is a difference between one rather dismal day and feeling like this all the time. If you find these feelings becoming a regular part of your working day once you are back then you'll need to be clear whether it is due to:

- not being given recognition for your contribution or
- not being paid enough or
- not being sufficiently stretched or challenged

Pay, recognition and responsibility are key motivators but your manager is not a mind reader so if this becomes an issue for you then a well timed 1 to 1 meeting to get it out on the table will help your manager know that you are dissatisfied. You'll need to offer suggestions that would turn the situation around and give your manager a chance to consider and implement these suggestions or come back with alternatives.

3) Wanting more time with your child

Toni talked about being on a treadmill and having too little quality time with her son after her return to work. Ultimately it was Toni's desire to give more of her time to her son as he grows up with Aspergers that led her to change career. Many mums who go back to work find themselves longing for more time with their baby. For some women it is a strong but temporary feeling that they get every now and then but on the whole they know they are working the right number of hours for their situation and their child is happy in childcare. The first mum interviewed in this book, Julie, is a good example here. Other mums find that their longing to spend more time with their child is more of a constant ache that of itself means a re-think about their working pattern is needed. This was a factor for Cerys who was determined that she wanted to be able to drop off and collect her son as he started primary school. Cerys changed job and employer to be able to do this. Only you will know where you sit on this spectrum once you have gone back to work and you will need to give it between 3 and 6 months to get an objective measure for your position.

4) Changing career

Please forgive me if this section is a bit long but this is an area that many mums spend time thinking about and for that reason it deserves more page space.

Toni's example shows that if you want to change career badly enough then anything is possible! Of course re-training for a total change of career is not without short term costs. Without Toni's salary the disposable income in her family has dropped sharply and added to this they need to cover the cost of childcare for Samuel while she is re-training. This is a stretch. Toni keeps her eyes on the prize however and knows that re-training is a means to achieving a part-time working solution that will meet her families needs in the future.

If you find that a change of career is your preferred route to a better work / family balance then you'll need to take time to think through what you want to do and what benefits you are seeking from the change. I think Toni really hits the nail on the head when she says that she felt as though she was a teenager all over again during this phase of her career change. Let's read her words again.

> "This was the first time in my life where I thought:
>
> You know, actually, my plan is no good anymore. I need a new plan!
>
> . . . suddenly I was 34 years old without a plan. No income, no job and no plan! And actually not having a plan was the scariest bit."

Do you remember what we learned from Dr Susan Jeffers in Part 1? When we seriously consider doing something new then it can cause us to feel afraid. In future you may find that changes at work or at home have tipped you off balance but you are scared to tackling the problem. Remember that feeling afraid of making big change, even towards something you hope will be better, is quite natural. Don't let fear keep you miserable.

While this book cannot cover all the options available to mums seeking part-time work in a new direction I will mention just a few to get you thinking but I'm sure you can readily think of others that are more suited to your experience, your talents, your passion and your financial requirements.

a) Don't overlook the obvious – your current employer

Employers committed to retaining talent will be open to discussing lateral moves for part-time workers. Before you decide to leave your current company investigate internal options that might provide the fresh challenge or the change that you are looking for. A friend of mine, Christina, returned to work after maternity leave in 2010 and now works 3 days a week. She rang me a few weeks ago to tell me that she is about to move from the Marketing department of her company to cover a role in the HR department while a colleague is on maternity leave. This will give her a fresh perspective on a business she has worked in for years and will be valuable experience, at an appropriate level, if she decides that a permanent move into HR is for her. Before you jump ship make sure you have a conversation with your employer about internal possibilities first. This might include:

-   a lateral (sideways) move into a different role
-   creating a job share opportunity from your current role

For further valuable information about creating a job share proposal go to www.capabilityjane.com for free downloadable information.

b) Look for part-time work on specialist websites

If you are adamant that you need a change of environment and want to look outside your current employer then websites such as www.capabilityjane.com or www.timewise. co.uk offer quality part-time and flexible roles. A growing number of enlightened employers are using sites such as these to recruit for part-time and flexible vacancies at all levels. These sites are certainly worth a visit and provide you with a chance to post your CV for employers to view.

c) Investigate franchise opportunities

If you have money to invest and want to run your own business then you might decide to invest in a franchise.

During your maternity leave you have probably met other mums who have gone down this road and are now running baby related businesses. Broadly speaking, the benefit of a franchise is that franchisees have the support of a national head office but the freedom to grow their business as they wish. In order to make this option work you will need lots of energy, a huge amount of commitment and be prepared to work the hours needed to support every aspect of a small business. You would also be well advised to ensure you have a business mentor who can give you the advice you will need both before and during your journey down this road. The grid in the section below for the self employed applies equally to those running a franchise.

d) Consider self employment

Becoming self employed is very different to being an employee. It needs careful consideration and, as with the franchise opportunity, I would strongly recommend that you find a business mentor to talk with before making any big decisions. Many people harbour a desire to work for themselves and hear wonderful stories about Mum-preneurs setting up home based businesses doing something they love and carving a niche that brings in a profit and fits around family life. In reality the women behind these success stories would be the first to point out that there are pros and cons to this work choice just as there are to being an employee. Here are a few:

Self employed Good Day	Self employed Bad Day
Workload is varied, challenging and changes everyday	Workload is overwhelming. You are M.D. through to cleaner
Exciting	Scary
Able to make own decisions	Have to make tough decisions
Freedom to succeed	Responsible for mistakes
Personal growth and achievement	Financial insecurity

No internal politics, get things done	Lonely, no one to talk to
Flexible hours that fit around family	Long hours that do not fit around family
Keep the profits	Responsible for losses
Ownership of assets	Cash investment up front – self funded

Although many mums will privately admit to considering resigning in order to start their own business far fewer actually take the plunge. If this option seems appealing then it might be exactly the right route for you. Only you can decide. Talking to someone who has gone down this road and is self employed would certainly be worthwhile. The government website www.gov.uk has a wide selection of resources available to help you to learn more about what this route involves. Some businesses start on a very small scale, perhaps as an evening or weekend venture, and subsequently grow into a bigger more viable work alternative.

Shelley, another contributor, was employed as a Buyer for a global automotive manufacturer before her children arrived. After the birth of her second baby she re-trained and set up as a self employed registered childminder so she could be at home and earn money while her children were small. She quickly became busy looking after the maximum number of children that regulation allowed. Despite the noise, chaos and house-turned-upside-down she enjoyed that phase of her career enormously and is rightly proud that her childminding business helped to pay for the two storey extension on her house.

The simplest route into self employment may not come through re creating the wheel but simply continuing to do what you have always done but on a consultancy basis registered as a sole trader. Hannah, the frustrated surveyor that I referred to earlier, has not looked back since she resigned and set up on her own as a sole trader. When asked what advice she would give to other mums who feel a change of job or career is what they need she said:

> "If, in the end, the working pattern you go back to doesn't work out then change it. Tell your employer that it's not working, move roles or companies, but don't put up with it because it's not good for anybody. If you are bright and intelligent and well qualified you will always find something else to do even if, in the interim, it may not be exactly what you want. I was prepared to do something temporarily to keep the money coming in. Just don't stick with something that doesn't work or makes you unhappy.
>
> Working for myself isn't always easy. There are times when I wonder if the work will come in and whether there is enough work for me to do. Am I earning enough? Is this sustainable? However, if you keep in touch with people and keep your network going then things do suddenly appear and there are opportunities out there to do different things."

We all know that the grass is not always greener on the other side and there is cow muck in every field but if you are ready for a new challenge then it can be truly re-energising. For more information on setting up as a sole trader go to www.gov.uk.

Where is Toni now?

Toni has taken a short break in her training to accommodate Bryson's needs but she is on track with her studies and is meeting required standards to qualify. She is due to start a four month teaching placement in a secondary school in autumn 2013. Once Toni has qualified she plans to complete a 12 month full-time paid placement as a chemistry teacher. By the end of 2015 Toni hopes to be in a position to apply for part-time teaching roles or become a self employed part-time tutor.

Summary of Part 5

Part 5 provided reassurance and outlined the options available if you receive a 'No' to your part-time working request. In this scenario your employer's decision may be disappointing but this section encouraged you not to jump to conclusions or take the decision personally. If you find yourself in this situation do make an appointment to go and discuss the content of the decision letter with your manager and see what the next steps are from their perspective. You might be surprised, as I was!

Cerys' interview demonstrated that if the 'No' means you are only able to go back to your current role full-time then you may need to take further action (perhaps in a different role or with different employer) to secure the part-time working pattern you want.

Emma's interview addressed the scenario that your part-time working pattern does not deliver or stops delivering the work / family balance intended. Emma suggested that regardless of what has caused the balance to deteriorate your first step ought to be a conversation with your manager. It may be all that is needed to reach agreement on an adjusted working pattern or a role change.

When major changes at home or at work mean that a complete re-think is needed the advice from Toni was to give yourself the time you need create your new plan and to remember that the scariest part of the change process is not having a plan. You will discover a way through your immediate challenge and if your new plan doesn't work out, think some more and change it again.

Getting back on track or finding an entirely new path requires adaptability and perseverance. If you can combine both of these and courageously pursue a solution that works for you as an employee and as a mum, you will keep your work / family balance intact as time passes.

Closing Words of Encouragement

As I sit here writing these final words my daughter, now aged 3, has joined me at the kitchen table to count her soft cheese triangles. We bought a big pack of them at the weekend. My table will shortly be covered with 16 slightly squished silver triangles and she will definitely need my help to put them back in the pack. We don't think twice about helping our children when they need it. Going back to work after maternity leave is a time when you need help and support too.

However you decide to use what you have read here and whether or not you actually do create:

- a part-time working request
- a re-integration support proposal
- a home support plan

I hope that you feel enlightened and encouraged to pursue the working pattern that you feel will best suit this season of your life. It is, after all, only a season and it will pass and life will move on.

Imagine yourself 12 months from now, settled and happy in your new routine with a successful part-time working pattern. Your baby will be in an even more vocal and mobile phase of development. You will have made a noticeable and positive contribution in your workplace and received praise for the part you have played. The money you earn will be helping your family and restoring your sense of self. You may even decide to set up a return-to-work buddy scheme to support other mums who are about to go through the return to work experience. In short, you will have "handled it"!

Your imagination is a powerful force that can pull you towards your future so whatever picture you have in your head of your part-time work / family balance, hang on to it and take action towards it, just as the women in these interviews have done.

All that remains is for me to wish you success in your discussions with your manager. I am confident that you will experience a positive return to work and hope that you really do enjoy every last minute of your maternity leave.

"Go confidently in the direction of your dreams - live the life you have imagined!"

- Henry David Thoreau (1817 - 1862)

End Notes

p.xi, *According to the Office for National Statistics 808,000 babies were born in the UK in 2011*: Report can be found on www.ons.gov.uk. Reproduced under Open Government Licence which can be viewed online at www.nationalarchives.gov.uk/doc/open-government-licence.

p.11, *Any time that you take a step in an unknown direction... you are going to feel fear. The only way to get rid of the fear of doing something is... do it!*: Susan Jeffers, "Feel the Fear and Do It Anyway®" Published by Century. Reprinted by The Random House Group. Reproduced here by permission of Mark Shelmerdine, CEO, Susan Jeffers, LLC. Further titles by Susan Jeffers can be found online at www.susanjeffers.com.

p.12, *If we take it to the very bottom line, the fear that you all have is that you won't be able to handle whatever life hands you*: Susan Jeffers, "Feel the Fear and Do It Anyway®" Published by Century. Reprinted by The Random House Group. Reproduced here by permission of Mark Shelmerdine, CEO, Susan Jeffers, LLC.

p.12, *I'll handle it*: Susan Jeffers, "Feel the Fear and Do It Anyway®" Published by Century. Reprinted by The Random House Group Limited. Reproduced here by permission of Mark Shelmerdine, CEO, Susan Jeffers, LLC.

p.19, *The Chatterbox in our minds ...tries to drive us crazy. It is the repository of all our negative input*. Susan Jeffers, "Feel the Fear and Do It Anyway®" Published by Century. Reprinted by The Random House Group. Reproduced here by permission of Mark Shelmerdine, CEO, Susan Jeffers, LLC.

p.32, A legal perspective: This section contains legislation from The Employment Rights Act 1996. Reproduced under Open Government Licence which can be viewed online at www.nationalarchives.gov.uk/doc/open-government-licence.

p.37, *In rejecting a flexible working request*: Extract from www.gov.uk/flexible-working/after-the-application Reproduced under Open Government Licence which can be viewed online at www.nationalarchives.gov.uk/doc/open-government-licence.

p.137, Employment Tribunal Claim figures quoted from HM Courts and Tribunal Service in response to a Freedom of Information request by the CIPD dated May 2012.

p.182, Contains extracts from Government Consultation Paper entitled 'Consultation on Modern Workplaces'. Paper can be viewed at www.gov.uk/government/uploads/system/uploads/attachment_data/file/34691/12-1269-modern-workplaces-response-flexible-working.pdf. Reproduced under Open Government Licence which can be viewed online at www.nationalarchives.gov.uk/doc/open-government-licence.

Appendices

A future legal perspective

The UK Government is planning to introduce changes to flexible working from around 2014. The changes are expected to be expansive rather than restrictive. Please find below an extract from the Government's consultation paper available online at www.gov.uk. Search for 'Consultation on Modern Workplaces: Government Response on Flexible Working'.

Summary of policy intention, page 7

Following analysis of the feedback the Government has concluded that it should proceed with the extension of the right to request flexible working to all employees and implement a package of measures to reform the right to request flexible working regulations. This will contribute to the Government's commitment to make the UK's employment practices more flexible and family-friendly. The key elements of this package will be to:

- Extend the right to request flexible working to all employees.
- Replace the current statutory procedure, through which employers consider flexible working requests, with a duty on employers to deal with requests in a reasonable manner, and within a *reasonable* period of time.
- Create a statutory code of practice to give guidance as to the meaning of 'reasonable' to employers.
- Provide guidance to employers on how to prioritise conflicting requests when received at the same time within the current framework for the right to request flexible working.
- Retain the 26 weeks qualifying period of continuous employment.

Government Next Steps, page 30

The next steps following the publication of the consultation paper include:

- Consulting on the Code Of Practice (2013)
- Implementation (2014)

It is heartening to learn who is involved in the creation of this new legislation. The consultation paper advises on page 15 that . . .

The Government has asked ACAS (Arbitration and Conciliation Advisory Service) to develop the Code of Practice and they have agreed.

The Private Sector Working Group on Flexible Working is working in an advisory role to support the development of the Code of Practice. The Group chaired by Sarah Jackson, Chief Executive of Working Families, brings together a range of experts . . . in order to generate practical ideas and outputs to encourage greater availability of flexible working and specifically looking at how to encourage flexible working in recruitment.

The intention of the new legislation appears to be:

- to enable all employees with 26 weeks continuous employment to apply for flexible working
- to make the flexible working application process easier to administer for employers
- to retain all the effective aspects of the current legislation
- to make the definition of 'reasonable' clearer for everyone

This ought to be good news for all concerned but what is this likely to mean for mums?

It does mean that flexible working applications might increase beyond 2014 and employers may need to choose which applications they prioritise.

The current requirement to have 26 weeks employment before making an application will remain.

The current restriction that only allows one flexible working application to be made in every rolling 12 months will remain.

The Government is considering extending the employer consideration period from 28 days to a maximum of 3 months. I understand this is in response to employer's concerns about the increased volume of applications. I believe this is unnecessary and will create specific disadvantages for mums on maternity leave. I sincerely hope the Government decides not to implement this part of the proposal and I have written to lobby against it.

There will still be a requirement for mums to think carefully about what they request and to negotiate effectively.

Once the revised legislation is in place then we will gain further clarity regarding any changes to;

- the process for employees in making an application
- the process for employers in considering applications
- the timelines for processing applications
- additional legislation to promote flexible working and flexible recruitment

Clearly in the not too distant future books such as this will need some revision however much of the advice offered here will remain useful well beyond the changes indicated. Keep an eye on www.gov.uk to stay up to date.

Index

Lightning Source UK Ltd.
Milton Keynes UK
UKOW02f1301030315

247201UK00015B/542/P